Praise for *Downfall* and Andrew Hacker

"The statistics Hacker provides are always revealing and often downright shocking."

—*Washington Post*

"Andrew Hacker has written a provocative book predicting a Trump defeat in 2020. And it goes beyond Trump to address changes in American society and politics that have influenced the current turmoil in the United States. Book discussion groups will be debating its contents right up to November and beyond."

—Joel D. Aberbach, Distinguished Professor Emeritus of Political Science and Public Policy, UCLA

"Few people writing today for a general audience can make more sense of numbers."

—*Wall Street Journal*

"Hacker's calm, analytical eye, his unblinking view of American history, and his unwillingness to accept cast and 'common sense' as facts."

—*The New York Times*

"In an area dominated by polemics, disingenuousness or the Saharan aridity of academic prose, Hacker invites us into his den for a quiet and richly documented conversation."

—*Boston Globe*

"Quietly terrifying."

—*Christian Science Monitor*

"Hacker's accounting of American history is knowledgeable, his judgments on it are just."

—*TIME*

"Accurate, incisive, never dull."

—*Times* Literary Supplement

"Perceptive, sharp, and stimulating."

—*Atlanta Journal*

DOWNFALL

DOWNFALL

THE DEMISE OF A PRESIDENT AND HIS PARTY

ANDREW HACKER

Skyhorse Publishing

Skyhorse Publishing books may be purchased in bulk at special discounts for sales promotion, corporate gifts, fund-raising, or educational purposes. Special editions can also be created to specifications. For details, contact the Special Sales Department, Skyhorse Publishing, 307 West 36th Street, 11th Floor, New York, NY 10018 or info@skyhorsepublishing.com.

Skyhorse® and Skyhorse Publishing® are registered trademarks of Skyhorse Publishing, Inc.®, a Delaware corporation.

Visit our website at www.skyhorsepublishing.com.

10 9 8 7 6 5 4 3 2 1

Library of Congress Cataloging-in-Publication Data is available on file.

Cover design by Mona Lin
Cover photo credit: Getty Images

Print ISBN: 978-1-5107-6019-6
Ebook ISBN: 978-1-5107-6020-2

Printed in the United States of America

Some material in Chapter 12 has appeared in *Bloomberg Opinion*.

For
Claudia and Ann
Betsy and Tim

CONTENTS

ACKNOWLEDGMENTS

My experience at Skyhorse Publishing again brought home to me how vital editors are to the literary craft. Hence my gratitude to Mark Gompertz, Elena Silverberg, Susan Barnett, Kirsten Dalley, and Mona Lin. They took my offbeat proposal seriously, reined me in when I bit off too much, and piloted nebulous drafts into an actual book.

At earlier stages, I had invaluable and expert assistance from Sydney Beveridge and Ann Gower. This is my seventh book with Robin Straus, who is far more than an agent. A cherished friend, she cheered me on through *Downfall*'s longer-than-usual gestation.

And, of course, my family. That's them in the Dedication.

When friends, colleagues, and acquaintances learned about the subject of this book, it often commandeered the conversation. Their questions, comments, even angst and disbelief, helped me at every stage. So my appreciation to:

Jorge Alves, Philip Anderson, Stewart Berger, John Bowman, Julia Cass, Robin Chotzinoff, Alyson Cole, Cory Dean, Eric Dexheimer, Joel Dreyfuss, Susana Duncan, Kathy Eden, Gwen Engelhard, Edward Jay Epstein, Ziva Flamhaft, Ellen Frell, Ester Fuchs, Julie George, Bill Goldstein, Ellen Gould, Timothy Gower, Lewis Gould Vartan Gregorian, David Helfand, Kenneth Hollander, Harvey Jay, Joseph Kanon, Andrew Katzenstein, Ethel Klein, Michael Krasner, Edward Krugman, Jon Landsman, Charles Lesage, Julia Lesage, Richard Levy, Peter Liberman, Sara Liberman, Judith Kimerling, Kenna Lipsitz, Karen Litzy, Ian Lustbader, Alda Muyskens, Jim Muyskens, Anne Nelson, Donald Newhouse, Nancy Newhouse, Dennis Overbye, Veronica Polland, Eduardo Porter, Patricia Rachal, FrancoisPierre-Louis, Alex Reichl, Sam Roberts, Ann Rolett, Rod Rolet, Joe Rollins, Daniel Rose, Don Rose, Joanna Rose, Rich Sandomir, Anya Schiffrin, Joan Silvers, Debora Spar, Joseph Stiglitz, Judith Summerfield, Yan Sun, Owan Tulloch, Daniel Victor, Diane Wachtell, Shelley Wanger, Nancy Wartik, Blake West, and Hratch Zadoian.

TO THE READER

It is unusual for a book to open with a missive like this. But *Downfall* is not a usual book.

As its subtitle proclaims, it offers a prediction. Even more, it does so with full confidence about what will occur. In this case, how millions of Americans will cast their ballots on this coming November 3. That forecast will be based on new and often unexpected findings about this nation's electorate.

But there's one piece of information that was not known when this book went to press. Democrats had yet to settle on their candidate. By some lights, this might seem a vital variable.

This year, it won't matter.

A central finding of *Downfall* is that whoever heads the Democratic ticket will crush Donald Trump. That entrant will win, simply by being an alternative to the current incumbent. Ensuing chapters will show the depth of public disgust, even in surprising parts of the country. Not to mention that Trump's 2016 following, far from growing, has severely diminished. In short, the casino magnate's trajectory is over. He can no longer lure enough Americans to swing the Electoral College, let alone a popular majority. As voters move down the ballot, they will unseat Republicans at every level. That party will pay the price of embracing him.

—A. H.

PART I
WHY HE CAN'T DO IT AGAIN

1
ONE TERM

There is not even a long-odds chance that Donald Trump will gain a second term. Nor is this wishful thinking. Compelling evidence abounds that anyone the Democrats nominate will win the popular vote, and by a margin to easily carry the Electoral College. Republicans down the ballot will suffer a similar demise, losing even more House seats, and very likely the Senate.

The chapters that follow, based on reliable facts and figures, will show how this upheaval is inevitable. Here are some signposts, to show how the book will unfold.

- In a shrouded symbiosis, Donald Trump and the Republican Party have been fueling their dual downfall. Both have become willfully insensible to how the bulk of their fellow citizens see themselves and feel about the world. A distinctive electorate is emerging, reflecting their own evolution and social trends, with new outlooks and attributes altering the political scene.
- Needless to say, the catalyst is the president himself. For more than four years, we have heard about the fervor and loyalty of his putative "base." What has more recently emerged is that this cadre ("Lock Her Up!") is dwindling rather than gaining new recruits. Attention will also be paid to his party, which is more than ever estranged from the rest of the country.
- It's not enough to record that most Americans "disapprove" of Donald Trump. True, they've been saying that to pollsters even before he took the oath. Subsequent voting has revealed something deeper. Our forty-fifth president evokes a revulsion unmatched in living memory. It's what is impelling the electoral surge aimed at his unseating.

- A recurring source for this book will be how Americans have been voting. Polls and interviews have their place, and will be used when they add to our understanding. But voting is special. It is a physical act, even if filling out a form and putting an envelope in the mail. Or it can call for planning out a day, waiting on line, possibly in the rain. When citizens take the effort to vote, it shows they're serious. We'll be listening.

- Donald Trump placed second in 2016, running 2,984,757 votes behind Hillary Clinton. As the world knows, he won via the Electoral College, by being 77,744 ahead in three key states. The odds against such a permutation occurring again are too high to fit on this page. His only hope for reelection is to enhance his total to win the popular count.

- This isn't going to happen. A welter of sources will be cited. Most compelling were the 2018 midterms, especially the races for the House of Representatives. On paper, ballots were cast for candidates for its 435 seats. In fact, the reason people showed up was to vent their feelings about the president. Here's how an eminent political scientist, Alan Abramowitz of Emory University, put it. "The 2018 midterm election was, to an extraordinary degree, a referendum on the presidency of Donald Trump."[1] Those supporting him did so by voting for whatever Republicans were on the card. Similarly, those who sought to oust him went straight to the Democratic column, often without reading the name of the candidate.

- Not only did the GOP lose the House. More arresting, 2018 saw a 12,225,230-vote plunge from Trump's 2016 showing. Even if all those absentees return in 2020, they won't be enough to swing the presidency for him.

- The pool of Americans primed to vote Democratic is its broadest and deepest since Barack Obama battered John McCain. In 2016, all too many of them weren't roused by Hillary Clinton and sat it out. But in 2018, enough of them emerged to make it the party's highest midterm showing since 1932. Their antipathy to the president will be just as fervid in 2020.

- Old rules don't apply. Like the mantra that material prosperity favors the party in power. (In fact, fewer people are thriving; wages lag behind executive bonuses and capital gains.) In 2018, candidates touched expected bases, like health costs, immigration, and mass shootings. But, as noted, it was primarily a plebiscite on a president and an early act of repudiation.

- True, a president can lose the House of Representatives at midterm and recover two years later. Obama did in 2010 and 2012, as Bill Clinton had in 1994 and 1996. Trump's problem is that his party has a hard time mustering presidential majorities. (They last did in 2004, against a hapless John Kerry.)
- Voting tells a larger story. Ballots are expressive of who we are and where our lives are going. Each year sees the nation mutating at an accelerating pace.[2] We know what's in the mix. There's more racial diversity and less identifying as heterosexual. College degrees are up, and birth rates are down.[3] So any forecast for 2020 must factor in how the parties are addressing a changing population.
- All indications are that Republicans are both unwilling and unable to see what's happening, let alone adapt to a shifting social scene. They have a lengthy platform, with avowals on abortion and firearms and military hegemony, plus veiled disquiet about the changing racial demographics of the country. But despite its details, it speaks inwardly, to a contracting following.
- Governors' races in 2018 and 2019 found Democrats winning, especially in unusual contests. In Kansas and Kentucky, the Republican entrants emulated Donald Trump in doctrine and demeanor. After all, he had carried those states by 20 percent and 30 percent. Their defeats attested that even stalwart Republicans were opening their minds. Louisiana's Democratic governor was reelected, boding that even the Deep South isn't safe for the GOP.
- Will money matter? It does in the primaries, for gaining recognition in a crowded field. It helps with chartering planes to waft you across Iowa, New Hampshire, and South Carolina. But not in general elections.[4] Hillary Clinton spent $768 million in 2016, while Donald Trump made do with $398 million, scarcely half as much. (Their per-vote quotients were $11.69 and $6.35.)[5] If money brings out votes, it should have yielded her either of Barack Obama's totals. Either of his edges would have precluded any problems with the Electoral College.
- Might the existence of this book undercut its forecast? In theory, some people might not take the trouble to vote if they believe the result is preordained. In fact, it doesn't happen that way. Citizens residing on the West Coast often hear how the rest of the country has tilted, but it

doesn't diminish their turnout. This year, more than any in most memories, people will line up to record their hopes and fears, if not forebodings of peril.

2
HOW WE GOT HIM

Primaries began as expressions of democracy. Presidential candidates were often culled by party bosses in proverbial smoke-filled rooms. To supplant these inner circles, the voting public would be given two opportunities to partake: at the nomination stage and then the general election. Tens of millions of citizens now turn out. In 2016, fully 60,542,136 lined up in the nominating cycle, as did 136,787,187 for the final balloting.

On Broadway, theaters conduct "casting calls." When a new production is underway, it's announced that anyone aspiring to a part can show up for an audition. And a similar sorting initiates how presidents are chosen. Thus the Republicans set a casting call for their first 2016 debate, to be held in August 2015 in Cleveland, a full fifteen months prior to the ultimate election. After preliminary gleaning, seventeen aspirants were deemed qualified for the event. Sixteen were men and one was a woman, a ratio reflective of the party's testosterone tilt. The panel included five sitting or former senators, nine past or present governors, a retired surgeon, and two business executives. Of the latter two, one was Carly Fiorina, the only woman, and the other Donald Trump.

Rewatching that initial August 2015 debate makes clear why Trump would surely finish first. What started to his advantage was the sheer size of the cast. Since the time given to each allowed barely a sound bite, attention would go the most arresting presence. Trump's fifteen seasons on *The Apprentice* obviously helped. To hold easily diverted viewers, television must make the most of every minute. Trump came prepared to dominate the stage with entrancing verbal tweets. Unlike the other sixteen, he felt no constraints regarding accuracy or civility, let alone paragraphs of policies.

Also bolstering him was the absence of a compelling rival. True, Republicans are not notable for charisma. In 2015, there certainly wasn't a nascent Dwight

Eisenhower or Ronald Reagan in the wings. An archetypal corporate favorite, Jeb Bush, was an early casualty, not least to Trump's ribald jibes.

The American presidency is an august institution and the GOP an esteemed association. To turn its selection process into so open an imbroglio is demeaning and self-defeating. Yet it isn't easy to propose a repair. What body would be empowered to tell a New Jersey governor or a South Carolina senator that their encumbering the platform would undermine common goals? Nor was there anyone to say that Donald Trump lacked the requisites for the Republican mantle.

Neither party could give a committee so encompassing a power. Lacking a protocol, both are tied to a volatile tiger, hurtled along whatever twists it takes.[1] Which is where Republicans found themselves when they saw their primaries giving their nomination to Donald Trump.

Unlike the other contenders, Donald Trump was a polished performer. Like all stars, he created his own following and never lost the spotlight. With the debates as spectacles and raucous rallies as his medium, he knocked off his opponents in quick succession.

Once he had joined the race, it's worth pondering whether his nomination was inevitable. There seem several reasons to think it was. As noted, he had no challenger with the stature of, say, Ronald Reagan. Established centers supported Jeb Bush a while, but he lacked the spirit or slogans to counterpunch Trump. The rest of the platform was easy pickings. The bottom thirteen, Carson through Perry, together amassed only 1,395,722 followers, not even a third of what Kasich drew by himself.

Mike Huckabee's paltry 51,947 and Rick Santorum's shameful 16,827 make clear they were never national figures. Insofar as their cluttering the platform paved the way for Trump, they served as spoilers on his behalf. True, the three runners-up, Cruz, Kasich, and Rubio, managed to assemble 15,504,654 votes. That was 1,941,410 over Trump's total, indeed a polling majority. Had they caucused, with two agreeing to step down, the third might have prevailed. Or perhaps not.

For practical purposes, the nation's parties are only shadows of their former selves. They were once disciplined associations, based on the loyalty of their adherents. True, there were regional and factional divisions. But when crucial choices had to be made, the watchword was in a venerable typing exercise: "Now is the time for all good men to come to the aid of their party."

They are still called parties, but they are no more than an ethereal presence. Both have national committees, with offices and staffs and fund-raising mailings. But they have been eclipsed by other entities. In the Republicans' case, think of the Kochs and the Mercers, the Chamber of Commerce, and the Club for Growth.[2]

There's another lesson of history. We can never foretell whether individuals will emerge to alter the course of events. Such a person was Donald Trump. To be sure, the full reckoning isn't in. Nor is it clear how lasting his imprint will be. Even so, his personal stamp on a national party has no recent rival.

No one sensed it beforehand, but 2016 was to become the most entertaining election in the nation's history. This was due, of course, to Donald Trump. (Bernie Sanders made his own contribution.) True, Ronald Reagan was also a performer. And he used the debates to his advantage. Even so, he had paid his partisan dues during two terms as governor of California, where he headed the nation's second-largest administration. Conceivably, it was only a matter of

AND THEN THERE WAS ONE			
1. Donald Trump	13,563,244	44.4%	Business owner
2. Ted Cruz	7,759,742	25.4%	Senator 2013–
3. John Kasich	4,230,697	13.8%	Governor 2011–2019
4. Marco Rubio	3,514,215	11.5%	Senator 2011–
5. Ben Carson	846,677	2.7%	Retired physician
6. Jeb Bush	286,680	0.9%	Governor 1999–2007
7. Rand Paul	67,795	0.2%	Senator 2011–
8. Chris Christie	58,377	0.2%	Governor 2010–2018
9. Mike Huckabee	51,947	0.2%	Governor 1996–2007
10. Carly Fiorina	41,077	0.1%	Retired executive
11. Jim Gilmore	18,418	—	Governor 1998–2002
12. Rick Santorum	16,827	—	Senator 1995–2007
13. Lindsey Graham	5,666	—	Senator 2003–
14. George Pataki	2,036	—	Governor 1995–2007
15. Bobby Jindal	222	—	Governor 2008–2016
16. Scott Walter	0	—	Governor 2011–2019
17. Rick Perry	0	—	Governor 2000–2015
All Others	120,182	0.4%	
	29,646,417	100.0%	

time before an ego like his would choose to use the nominating process as a personal pedestal.

That Donald Trump won his party's nomination was far from being fortuitous. It was due to his hard and unrelenting effort. Thus he outflanked and outperformed his rivals, not least by rewriting the rules for how that prize should be secured. (Think back on how conventionally Mitt Romney and John McCain attained their candidacies.)

The general election proved to be a different story. From one standpoint, Trump reached the Oval Office due to a historic happenstance. It was that 1789 and 1804 essentially set in stone an entity called the Electoral College, whose members have the final say on who will be the nation's chief executive. Trump pinned down 304 of its 538 votes, in the only computation that counts.

Did He Win, or Did She Lose?

From another vantage, it could be contended—as it will be here—that Donald Trump did not win the presidency. Rather, Hillary Rodham Clinton lost it.

Why she bombed has been much discussed and will long be debated. The litany includes missing emails, insinuations by the FBI, closed conclaves with financiers, not visiting Wisconsin. She also found herself facing an opponent who outmatched her in vigor and verve, not to mention a single-sentence message. Plus how she seemed to come across: aloof, stolid, the favored student. What prospect, if any at all, was she pledging for the country?[3]

Even amid differences in style, Trump and Clinton shared at least one trait. It was a feeling of *entitlement*. Trump could get away with it, by brazening out any imbroglios. As with secreting his taxes, or fabricating bone spurs to cloak his cowardice, Clinton's demeanor sent a not-dissimilar message. It was that it was her turn to have the presidency. What came across was that she had paid her dues, which warranted her return to the White House. Of course, such presumptions are seen as less tenable in a woman. Trump could refuse to answer charges by just jutting his chin. Clinton may have felt entitled, but she couldn't match her opponent in arrogance. At any event, her choice to obfuscate her Wall Street speeches factored in her defeat.

No one would call Donald Trump a philosopher. But don't be so quick on that score. He presented himself as articulating a vision for his nation and its citizens. To be sure, it was succinct enough to fit on a cloth cap. Yet the fact was that "Make American Great Again" struck chords with lots of people, as did his even terser "America First!" Moreover, this was Trump's personal credo.

His America would have a supra-strong military and an economy that would stare the world down.

It was not just that Clinton lacked a pithy slogan. ("Stronger Together" could have announced a new glue.) She wasn't the kind of individual who entertains visionary thoughts and dreams. Hence she could only advance what she herself was, a policy wonk who would replicate the texture and tenets of Barack Obama's popular, if not very inspiring, administration. But even there, she couldn't replicate Obama's subdued but good-humored spirit. Compared with both Trump and Obama, Clinton emerged as quite ordinary. Yet she couldn't be other than what she was.

Nor did Clinton lose because Trump ran a winning campaign. In fact, he attracted a smaller share of the popular total than Mitt Romney, who failed to unseat Obama in 2012. She lost because she failed to enlist men and women who had quite recently shown a willingness to vote Democratic. They were there, in every state, waiting to be lured. They weren't like the Republicans who truly detested Clinton. They would have been willing to show up for her, if she had given them some reasons to.

And we know the size of that pool. In 2008, it was 69,498,459, the number of people who had turned out for Barack Obama. More to the point, they were Americans who showed themselves willing to vote for a Democrat, indeed one with an exotic name and an African parent. Almost all of them were still around in 2016, joined by new voters. Between 2008 and 2016, the number of Americans eligible to vote increased by a bit over 8 percent. If we adjust Obama's 2008 turnout to match the 2016 electorate, there were 75,128,851 potential Democrats out there in 2016.

Yet, as we know, Clinton's majority was 65,677,168. That puts her 9,275,129 votes behind Obama's first try. (And 3,067,914 less than his 2012 reelection victory.) The hard fact is that relatively few of the missing Obama people veered to Donald Trump. The great majority simply stayed at home. In their view, there just wasn't enough about Clinton to make going to the polls worth their while.

3
THOSE THREE STATES

If Clinton had matched even Obama's 2012 margin, those added votes would have been more than enough to carry Pennsylvania, Wisconsin, and Michigan and swing the Electoral College to her. Strategists in Hillary Clinton's campaign should have had the states' 2008–2014 figures, as seen below, posted prominently in their cubicles. They well knew that the three states it depicts were crucial battlegrounds. Their twelve numbers carried ominous messages.

Most visible was the inconstancy of Democratic voters in those states. Here are some warnings from four elections prior to 2016.

- In 2008, all three states went strongly for Obama, visibly ahead of the nation as a whole. Yet four years later, his margin was 939,895 lower, while Republicans were improving their edge. This isn't inevitable in reelection bids. Bill Clinton and George W. Bush did better their second time around. The short story was that Democrats were losing traction, less by defections to Republicans than that earlier supporters were staying at home.

- Despite Democratic majorities in 2008 and 2012, in the subsequent midterms, Republicans easily carried the three states. They managed this not by drawing from the other side, but by getting their own troops out. Only 54 percent of 2008 Democrats showed up in 2010, whereas a solid 82 percent of Republicans did. Turnouts were lower in 2014, but Republicans were sixteen points ahead.

WISCONSIN, MICHIGAN, PENNSYLVANIA: 2008–2016		
Democrats	2008	Republicans
7,816,158 (56%)	President	5,967,117 (43%)
Democrats Ahead: 1,909,041		
Democrats	2010	Republicans
4,236,094 (46%)	Midterm	4,871,613 (52%)
Republicans Ahead: 635,519		
Democrats	2012	Republicans
7,175,802 (53%)	President	6,206,656 (46%)
Democrats Ahead: 969,146		
Democrats	2014	Republicans
4,089,205 (47%)	Midterm	4,533,290 (52%)
Republicans Ahead: 444,085		

- In 2016, the states were not just in play, but were seriously at risk. The chief problem was somnolent Democrats. The party's tacticians must have known they had a less-than-popular candidate, necessitating a need to rouse latent loyalties. Yet even in a high-profile presidential year, they drew out only 78 percent of their 2008 pool. The parallel Republican rate was 97 percent. And it netted them their historic 77,744 margin.

4
EMBRACING AN INTERLOPER

Donald Trump brought to 2016 the brute force of visceral energy. Unlike any earlier entrant, his electric presence and unrivaled stamina literally steamrollered across the Republican primaries and the ensuing election. If he didn't win the popular count, he did almost as well as Mitt Romney had four years earlier, when growth of the electorate is factored in.

Central to Donald Trump's success was the hold he came to have over his party. His mantra of restoring American might played a key role. But just as crucial was that regular Republicans, on their own and ultimately collectively, found themselves accepting that he was their man. They tacitly agreed not to be deterred by his demeanor, even at its most outrageous. The first task for those who aspire to leadership is to amass a following. Donald Trump did that.

So Republicans who had rallied to Mitt Romney and John McCain chose not to be shocked by Trump's checkered history, demeaning behavior, and contempt for figures long loyal to the party. By now, the list is memorable. A sampling is provided below.

True, some Republicans were ill at ease, at least for a time. Evidence of this came from an unusual source. When approached by pollsters, a not-small portion who had decided to vote for him declined to admit that they would. Were they just a little ashamed, even on the phone in an anonymous interview? (These evasions were much of the reason why surveys showed Clinton ahead.) But by November, reluctance and hesitation had vaporized. Regular Republicans chose to see him as an errant member of the household, even while wincing at his assaults.

The table below highlights this continuity. Results from a cross section of states shows how Mitt Romney's and Donald Trump's 2012 and 2016 followings were almost identical. It's important to add that the two elections had similar defection rates. CNN exit polls in both years and for both parties

WHAT REPUBLICANS CHOSE TO IGNORE

- Donald Trump's blithe refusal to release his tax returns.
- That various of his ventures ended in bankruptcy, leaving his investors, suppliers, and workers with the bulk of the bills.
- Tapes showing him bragging of assaulting women.
- Three marriages, interleaved with infidelities.
- Hiring overseas workers for his resorts and importing construction materials.
- Evading military service by citing a dubious disability.
- Revealing no religious inclinations, attendance, or affiliations.
- Continual insinuations that a recent president was not native born.
- Refusing to cast himself as *conservative*, long expected for Republican aspirants.
- Brutally ridiculing his primary opponents, despite their impeccable party credentials.
- Mocking John McCain for his capture during the Vietnam War.
- Deriding the previous GOP president for invading Iraq.
- Calling climate change a hoax and a ruse by China to gain trade advantages.
- Voicing admiration for Vladimir Putin, Russia's autocratic premier.
- Dubbing his opponent "Crooked Hillary" and smirking at roars of "Lock Her Up!"

showed just about 8 percent crossed over, a customary quotient.[1] Much has been made of Democrats who switched to Trump. Romney had recruited just as many.

The atmosphere at Trump's rallies during the primaries and general campaign was unlike that ever observed at Republican gatherings. The walls resounded with cries for blood. A common explanation was that most of them were blue-collar newcomers, a bit coarser than the older guard, arriving in denim shirts and pickup trucks.

In fact the GOP resembles the Democrats in being a multiclass party. It has long had blue-collar echelons, notably along an arc stretching from South

Carolina to South Dakota.[2] While the party does well among the affluent, its adherents are less likely to be college graduates. Most of the states Republicans carry do little to encourage education. So this stratum was not newly co-opted by Trump. It has always been there, augmented when the party absorbed the former Confederacy.

CONTRASTING CANDIDATES, COMPARABLE SUPPORT		
	Romney	Trump
Arkansas	62%	61%
South Carolina	55%	55%
Minnesota	45%	45%
Connecticut	41%	41%
Nevada	46%	46%
New Hampshire	46%	47%
Florida	49%	49%
Wyoming	69%	68%

Equally numerous were middle-class stalwarts who had, as noted, lined up for Mitt Romney, John McCain, and the two Bushes. They had basked in Ronald Reagan and endured Richard Nixon. And in all of these earlier campaigns, they had displayed the bearing of their luncheon clubs and golfing outings. If they were passionate about their party, in earlier elections they showed it by sedate applause rather than bellicose bellowing.

So it was the same stalwarts roaring, now in Trump's arenas. Apparently, these furies had long been repressed, waiting for a tribune to unleash them. Ironically, it awaited a self-aggrandizing New Yorker to expose an underside of Republican fealty, an edge not seen since its obsession with communist subversion six decades earlier.

Journalists and other observers, stunned by Trump's vulgarity, became convinced that many mainstream Republicans would be equally repelled. They were thinking of landscaped suburbs, soccer moms, and college-bound seniors. As noted, some of these denizens were initially hesitant about Trump. Yet as it became apparent that he would be their party's nominee and carry its banner in the campaign, insurance agents joined electricians in "Make America Great Again" caps and clamoring to "Build the Wall!" Most simply, Donald Trump would grasp the presidency for their party and sweep in the rest of the ticket. So there emerged an agreement to stomach him as he was, and not cavil over his bragging and bullying, even if it extended to sexual molestation.

There is another, less remarked, facet to browbeating. Recall schoolyard days, when youngsters who would later be dentists and accountants would seek a burly classmate as a protector. In a word, gain a safe haven behind their own bully. Or on the distaff side, toadying up to the mean girls, who took you into their clique, or at least its periphery. So another aspect of Trump's virtuosity was his understanding that a lot of people don't oppose intimidation. Rather, they want it on their behalf.

In the end, four of every ten women who cast ballots rejected the first-ever candidate of their gender. No less striking, they turned out for a man who belittled them as trophies or toys. To be sure, many liked his policy positions, like his long-held views on immigration and his newfound stance on abortion. This noted, other impulses may have abetted their decision. Some women are drawn to "bad boys," finding themselves falling for guys who break the rules, bringing a frisson of daring to routine lives. (It's a reason so many households are headed by women; these men make babies and move on.) If Trump made some men feel more manly, for some women he was an avatar of virility.

Not to mention the cheers when he boasted of evading taxes, an avowal no earlier candidate dared to emit. Yet even country-club Republicans might harken with admiration and envy. Could it be what they would themselves do, had they his audacity? The bad-boy magnetism can work on men as well. Main Street pillars were mesmerized by a crass Manhattan marketeer.

Another 2016 mantra was that Trump's supporters were angry. Indeed, they were depicted as more incensed than any audiences in living memory. One rendering was that many had been employed in well-paying work, and were no longer able to find the kinds of jobs they felt were their due. Hence their venting on Asian nations, for undercutting American manufacturing. Or on migrants from Mexico, who dragged down wages in such jobs as remained. Adding to the rage was seeing values they cherished being derided by arrogant elites. Hence rallies vibrated with cries, from building a wall to consigning a competing candidate to prison.

Yet it would be hard to show that this fury had been smoldering in the nation. The party's 2008 and 2012 campaigns neither disclosed nor released such rancor. On the contrary, they were stolidly sedate, albeit with a few riffs from Sarah Palin. All indicators showed that Republicans were living comfortably, signing up for Caribbean cruises and sojourns to Disney parks, and installing granite kitchens. Had a Rubio or Kasich or Cruz been nominated, 2016 would have been much the same.

Here's a test of whether a cadre of Republicans found Trump too crass for their tastes. Were that so, they might have left the presidential column blank, but would still have turned out for the rest of their party's races. Had that occurred, Trump would have run behind down-ballot Republicans.

But he didn't. In most states, Trump got essentially the same totals as the party's statewide and congressional candidates. In some, he did better. In Pennsylvania, he came in 19,031 votes ahead of his party's senatorial entrant. In Missouri, he garnered 161,114 more votes than its choice for governor.

So for all Trump's rough and raucous ways, Republicans soon decided they wanted him for their president. Not least, he satisfied their party's checklist: abortion, cutting taxes, guns, military might, slowing the nation's progress toward a diverse population. Above all, they saw him as a vehicle to put all branches of government under their control. On January 20, 2017, they had just that.

5

A PRESIDENTIAL CHEAT SHEET

- In the seventy-five years since the end of World War II, the country has had eighteen presidential elections, with twelve winning candidates. Of the victors, six have been Republicans and six were Democrats. Four of the Republicans won second terms. Four of the Democrats were also reelected, two of whom were Harry Truman and Lyndon Johnson, who moved up from vice president.
- This period also had seventeen defeated candidates. (Adlai Stevenson lost twice.) Of those losers, eight were Republicans and nine were Democrats. One of the Democrats who lost (Jimmy Carter) was a sitting president. So were two of the Republicans (Gerald Ford and George H. W. Bush).
- Of the nine defeated Democrats, only Carter was a sitting president. Three had been vice presidents: Hubert Humphrey, Walter Mondale, and Albert Gore. Nominating them was a tapestry of errors. All were desultory campaigners with no national appeal. The same was true of George McGovern, Michael Dukakis, and John Kerry. (Stevenson had telling wit, but was doomed to face a wartime hero.) While these defeated Democrats tried, their best wasn't enough. Ninth on this doleful list was Hillary Clinton. In ways, she resembled Stevenson and Carter, in having a larger-than-life opponent.
- There are lessons in Clinton's campaign. It turns out that being a woman didn't help her with women: 55 percent of them had voted for Obama in 2012, as 54 percent did for her. More glaring in the equation was that she ended *only* 2,984,757 votes ahead of Trump. As we know too well from 2000 and 2016, Democrats need an extra edge to offset the quirks of the Electoral College.
- Losing the House of Representatives couldn't have been cheering news for Donald Trump and his party. In theory, a recovery is possible. Barack

Obama lost the House in 2010 and went on to get reelected in 2012. Trump has to hope he can match that feat. To stay in the White House, Obama called on his 2008 supporters, who had provided one of the largest majorities in recent history. Trump doesn't have that kind of backstop. Indeed, the 2018 midterms made clear that his 2016 cadre has been dissolving.

- As the presses start rolling on this book, Democrats have yet to settle on their nominee. For simplicity's sake, I'll make do with two models. One would be a younger candidate, quite new to the national scene, as Obama was in 2008. The other would be older, with a familiar image and message. Neither would be a fatal choice. The reason is that an outsized majority is already eager to oust Donald Trump.

- It won't matter if the Democrats' candidate is to the left or gaffe-prone or a woman or unusually young. Even if some of these attributes prompt a little headshaking, they will not cause hesitant Democrats to vote for Donald Trump. At worst, some may sit it out, reducing the party's majority. But even that is unlikely, as was attested by the 93 percent turnout in 2018. Dread of another Trump term will override all uncertainties.

- For a deeper perspective, we'll journey back 160 years, to 1860, when Abraham Lincoln became the first Republican to win the White House. Including that election, the party has had twenty presidents, who together have had a varied electoral experience. Donald Trump's hopes can be set against that array. Most notable were the seven who won a first term and then another one. They were Abraham Lincoln, Ulysses Grant, William McKinley, Dwight Eisenhower, Richard Nixon, Ronald Reagan, and George W. Bush. (But Lincoln, McKinley, and Nixon didn't finish their second terms.)

- Two—Theodore Roosevelt and Calvin Coolidge—ascended from vice president and then won a full term on their own. Rutherford Hayes attained one term and decided not to run again. (He got that one with a lower popular total.) Four served part of one term. James Garfield and Warren Harding died in office. Andrew Johnson and Chester Arthur moved up from vice president, but didn't run when the rest of their tenure ran out.

- Gerald Ford also moved up from vice president, and was defeated when he ran on his own. Four served one full term and were defeated when they tried for reelection. They were Benjamin Harrison, William Howard Taft, Herbert Hoover, and George H. W. Bush. In sum, among the twelve presidents sharing Donald Trump's current prospect, seven won another term and five did not.

6
THE 93 PERCENT TURNOUT

Or, better, call it the 93 percent solution. We all know that Democrats captured the House of Representatives in the 2018 midterms. What's less widely understood is how they did it. Despite vote suppression and biased maps, they swept that chamber as their party hasn't since 1932.

What happened was that 93 percent of the Democrats' 2016 supporters turned out again twenty-four months later. That level of loyalty was both stunning and surprising.[1] Pundits mused that Democrats might win the House. But none foresaw that so many Americans would show up in an off year. Simply as bodies lining up, it was the highest midterm showing for any party ever. It was all the more notable because it was Democrats who did it.

Much is made of the fact that Hillary Clinton ended 2,847,757 votes ahead of Donald Trump. But the Democrats' 2018 margin, as expressed in House races, was 9,852,442, over three times Clinton's in 2016. In itself, this was notable. Parties are supposed to show their best in presidential years. To do even better when no national figure is atop the ticket means something momentous is afoot.

In the last seven presidential races, Democrats have won the popular count in six of them. So they can bestir themselves if they want to, as they did twice for Barack Obama and Bill Clinton. Yet for over a decade, they had been strangely somnolent in off-year elections. In 2010 and 2014, they could have come out to backstop the man they had put in the presidency two years earlier. Yet on both occasions, almost half of them chose to do other things on Election Day. As a result, Congress and most state capitols went to the GOP, giving the nation a rightward tilt, from which it's still reeling. In those midterms, Republicans were driven by party loyalty, plus a focus on firearms ownership and antipathy to abortion. In 2010 and 2014, Democrats had nothing so singular to spur them to the polls. But in 2018, they would.

Two quotients, readily derived from the table, add to the mix. Between 2016 and 2018, the number of Republicans who bestirred themselves to vote declined by 12,225,230, a high abstention rate for their party. In vivid contrast, the Democratic figure was less than half that, 5,357,545.

While there were several reasons for the high Democratic turnout, one stood well at the top. But it's not the one commonly cited. Or the one Democrats prepared for public consumption.

THE BIG SWITCH		
2016	**Who Showed Up**	**2018**
136,787,187	All Voters	114,016,831
65,677,168	Democrats	60,319,623
62,692,411	Republican	50,467,181
2,847,757	Democratic Lead	9,852,441
Midterm Turnouts *Percent of Previous Presidential Totals*		
Democrats		Republicans
56%	2010	74%
52%	2014	64%
93%	2018	81%

The Democratic story was that 2018 was like all midterms, scheduled to fill lesser offices, with the president absent from the ballot. Hence candidates should appeal to voters locally, as if Donald Trump had vaporized. Here was Nancy Pelosi's recounting. "We said to the candidates, 'Don't even mention his name. This is not about him.'" If she uttered this with a straight face—it was off-camera—she must have snuck in a wink. Everyone from Pelosi to county clerks knew that 2018 was a nationwide plebiscite on the personality and presidency of Donald John Trump. A total of 114,016,831 adults showed up—an all-time midterm high—ready to fill bubbles for whatever Republicans or Democrats they found on their local ballots.[2]

The best available study has found that only 37 percent of Americans can name the individual their district has sent to the House of Representatives. Fewer recall the losing challengers, including the person for whom they actually voted.[3]

Thus most Republicans who resided in New Jersey's 11th District didn't make the trip to vote for Jay Webber. As noted, it wasn't a name on their mental Rolodex. Rather, they were among the 50,467,181 Republicans who lined up to record their confidence in the president.

The same applies for the majority of Democrats who supported Mary Jennings Hegar in Texas's 31st district. They were among the 60,319,623 citizens who cast their votes for any Democrat, as their best way of saying that they wanted another president.

Nancy Pelosi's script stressed the candidates' expected agendas. Democrats would dilate upon health costs and gun control, while Republicans would hold forth on low taxes and unwelcome immigrants.

But it didn't matter whether or not they did. Those 114,016,831 voters, by their own choice and volition, brought Donald Trump with them into the booth. And by marking their ballots for Jay Webber or Mary Jennings Hegar, they were transcribing their verdict on the nation's chief executive.

So 2018 was a forerunner for 2020. As an ostensible plebiscite, it yielded 45 percent for retaining the president against 55 percent for removing him. Until the 2020 election eventuates, this is the best evidence we have of the mood of the nation.

One state told much of the story. Iowa was carried handily by Trump in 2016, with three of its four House seats also going to Republicans. In 2018, that ratio was totally reversed, with three of the four House seats captured by Democrats. Here's how that happened. The Democrats' 2018 turnout was actually higher—664,676 to 653,669—than in 2016, which is almost unheard of in a midterm. On the GOP side, fully 200,858 Trump voters sat 2018 out. Other Republican base states showed similar shrinkage.

Since Donald Trump's inauguration, polls have uniformly shown disapproval of his personality and performance. But they didn't capture how intensely the electorate felt about the man. People had their circles of friends; yet there was a huge nation out there. The decision to vote conveys far more than terse responses to interviewers. And a shattering 93 percent of Democrats made that effort. Nor is that engagement likely to ebb by 2020. Of course, Republicans will be turning out too. But if 2018 generally and Iowa in particular are previews, their party's curve isn't ascending. Quite the opposite.

7
KANSAS?

The first sign that Donald Trump was on a downward arc came only eighty-one days into his term. All it took was two numbers. They arrived a few minutes before midnight on April 11, 2017, on the website of the *Wichita Eagle*. They were:

64,004   56,435

For those who knew and cared, they signaled that something exceedingly unexpected had happened during that day.

Here's the backstory. These were the totals cast for the Republican and the Democrat vying in a special election for a Kansas congressional seat. The incumbent, Mike Pompeo, had resigned to be Donald Trump's head of the CIA, and later secretary of state. It had long been a solid Republican seat, where Wichita merges into wheat fields. Five months earlier in that district, Trump had ridden roughshod over Hillary Clinton by twenty-seven points. As anticipated, the new Republican replaced Pompeo.

But in politics as in sports, the scores are less important than the spread. What struck informed observers was that the Republican finished *only* 7,569 votes ahead. Democrats aren't supposed to come that close in Kansas. After all, this was a state which since 1939 has sent only Republicans to the US Senate. But the April 11 spread was a spindly seven points.

There were omens on both sides. The 56,435 votes for the Democrat meant that among those who had supported Clinton in 2016, an impressive 69 percent made time for the April election. Apparently, just eighty-one days of Donald Trump sufficed to propel them to the polls.

The 64,004 for the Republican was a more ominous portent. Those five digits attested that if they weren't ready to repudiate their president, enthusiasm for him was waning. Of those in the district who backed Trump in 2016, only 39 percent were moved to make the April vote. Put another way, fully 101,178 of them chose to do other things that day. That's not the way Republicans are supposed to behave, especially in Kansas. No less than voting, staying home sends a message. (A similar nonchalance would recur a year and a half later, in November 2018.)

8
IRREGULAR ELECTIONS

The surprising tally in Kansas came in as the first of thirteen special elections that would be held from April 2017 through September 2019. All were unexpected, not listed on any political calendar. So voters would need to hear about them on their own and post reminders on their refrigerator doors.

Due to resignations, twelve House seats held by Republicans, and one in the Senate, had fallen vacant. Some of the incumbents had joined the incoming administration, while others faced charges of sexual or kindred misconduct. Two of the thirteen, for the House in Montana and the Senate in Alabama, would be statewide contests.

Careful scrutiny of the first ten could have yielded clues as to how the parties would fare in the November 2018 midterms. One reason for the lack of probing was that all of these seats had been safely Republican, and their candidates ended retaining eleven of them, often by comfortable margins. One exception was the first of two Pennsylvania contests, where a Democrat named Conor Lamb slipped in by 627 votes.

The other Democratic victory, in Alabama, was a special case. The Republican, Roy Moore, had to cope with allegations of child molestation. Still, Doug Jones's successful run was his party's first statewide win in fifteen years. How and why he won can be rendered in two quotients. The first was that a remarkable 90 percent of Clinton voters came out for him. The second is that only 49 percent of Republicans showed up for Roy Moore. There's never been a contest where so many of the party's supporters—684,668 by my count—sat it out.

The sources of Jones's strength can be inferred from exit poll responses.[1] It emerged that his principal bloc was 367,933 black Alabamians, who were joined by 261,677 whites. This said, it should be noted that almost 70 percent of whites who marked ballots gave them to Moore. That Jones's lead was so

Republicans	SPECIAL ELECTIONS: 2017–2019	Democrats
	Turnouts Compared with 2016	
39%	Kansas (April 2017)	69%
101%	Montana (May 2017)	102%
28%	South Carolina (June 2017)	40%
67%	Georgia (June 2017)	101%
41%	Utah (November 2017)	50%
5%	Arizona (November 2017)	88%
49%	Alabama (December 2017)	90%
53%	Pennsylvania (April 2018)	80%
15%	Texas (June 2018)	16%
42%	Ohio (August 2018)	91%
44%	Pennsylvania (May 2019)	46%
35%	North Carolina (September 2019)	35%
51%	North Carolina (September 2019)	63%
48%	Average	67%

solidly brought by black voters was a landmark. But it was also an anomaly. After all, this is the state that gave Jeff Sessions 63 percent of its votes in his last contested election.

The best gauge of turnouts for special elections is a comparison with the most recent presidential contest, when the parties are energized and public attention is highest. The table above shows these ratios.

In four of them—Montana, Texas, and one each in North Carolina and Pennsylvania—involvement was about the same.[2] What stands out is how much higher the Democratic figures are in the other nine contests. That the Democrats lost seven of them is not at issue. What counts was how galvanized they were.

All the more, since these were states and districts where their party often comes in second. Of course, investing in swing states like Ohio, Arizona, Montana, and North Carolina makes sense. But signs of Democratic fortitude in South Carolina, Georgia, Utah, and Alabama suggest that the national mood is changing. That the Democrats' overall average was almost twenty points ahead attests that serious shifts were afoot.

It remains to wonder why Republican turnouts were lower—a forty-three-point gap in Arizona, forty-nine points in Ohio—especially in terrain Republicans ordinarily command.[3] Their party has been known for its loyalists, who can be relied on to rally, especially for less-publicized races.

Few will admit aloud that their fervor for Donald Trump is waning. Their staying home said it for them.

9
SURRENDERED SEATS

Another straw in the wind also evoked little or no comment. It was that the GOP, for the 2018 midterms, chose not to contest 38 of the 435 seats in the House of Representatives. It was one of the highest such rates in recent history.[1] (In 2016, they bypassed twenty-two races, against the Democrats' twenty-four.)

True, both parties have lists of seats they sense they cannot win. Today's districts tend to tilt heavily in one direction. If gerrymandering is one reason, spontaneous social clustering is also in the mix. Even so, the parties often make a try against harsh odds, as a way of proclaiming they embrace the entire nation.

One might think Republicans would want to convey an air of confidence in 2018, if only as a warmup for 2020. If appearances count, forsaking one in eleven of the House races doesn't auger a self-assured party. Among the thirty-eight were six in New York, eight in California, plus four in Texas, one of the Republican Party's flagship states.

The seats they gave up were revealing in another way. In twenty-three of the thirty-eight, the incumbent Democrats listed other than European origins. That the GOP is overwhelmingly white is no secret. (CNN's 2018 poll had that figure at 88 percent, against 54 percent for the Democrats.) What's less clear is whether the party wants to alter its racial ratio. It likes to showcase Clarence Thomas and Ben Carson, as well as its two senators of Cuban lineage. It would not have taken a huge effort to find some African American, Hispanic, and Asian conservatives to make the run. A $100,000 campaign chest for each would total $3.8 million, a sum the party could easily provide.

By my count, these empty ballots brought a 2,473,998 dip in the GOP's overall 2018 tally. As some citizens opted to stay home, a whole party was seen sitting out much of a national event. It betokened a lack of resolve, in many ways surprising for Republicans. In their 2010 sweep, they fielded candidates in 430 districts. At the time, that was the highest number ever.

The Democrats, in a notable move, decided to contest a record of 432 House seats. It signaled an urge to show the flag, no matter how forbidding the terrain. In an upcountry Texas district, an intrepid Greg Sagan notched 17 percent of the tally, with a total budget of $28,701. In its way, his 35,083 votes contributed to the turnout that gave Democrats their historic midterm margin.

Of course, not every seat is winnable. But impressions can be deceiving. Like an apparent Republican stronghold in Virginia, where a challenger named Dave Brat displaced Eric Cantor, the House minority leader, in a 2014 primary. In the ensuing election, Brat swamped his Democratic opponent by twenty-four points. Two years later, with Donald Trump on the ticket, Brat still led by sixteen points. Yet in 2018, a New Jersey transplant named Abigail Spanberger bested Brat by 6,784 votes. It was not the only constituency where a Trump connection had become a liability.

10
RALLYING THE FLOCK

When credit is due, it should be bestowed, even if the recipient is Donald Trump. Of the mantles conferred on presidents, not least is to serve as their party's leader. And this is more than a formality. It calls for joining the political rough-and-tumble; in particular, seeking to influence elections. After all, programs will only be enacted if there is support in legislative chambers. So it seems reasonable to expect that presidents will extend themselves to fill the needed seats. Yet it's revealing how rarely this occurs. It isn't easy to recall presidents who traversed the nation to aid colleagues at the polls. Until Donald Trump.

On forty-six mornings from March through November 2018, he flew from the White House, often to remote terrain, to ignite Republican rallies. Of course, these events were unabashedly partisan, thronged with friendly faces. Indeed, that was their point. These conclaves had a singular purpose: to loft the party's midterm aspirants. The sheer number of these occasions, heightened by his personal presence, was unique in presidential annals. No other chief executive of any party had invested that level of energy or commitment.

Barack Obama had this opportunity in 2010 in facing his first midterm, as had Bill Clinton in 1994. Both presidents had policies they sought to advance, for which they needed congenial spirits on Capitol Hill. Yet neither essayed anything like Donald Trump's grand tour. Whether for this reason or others, both lost their House majorities in their first midterm. (Clinton lost the Senate as well.) Trump had to be concerned that this could happen to him.

If his arenas were reserved for his faithful, the agenda was not just adulation. There was a practical intent. It was to rouse enough votes in 2018 for Republicans to keep full control of the Congress and state capitals. So Trump's entreaty to his audiences was to return home and urge friends and neighbors and anyone else to be at the polls on November 6. His tour would be a test of the extent and depth of his influence.

In all, the president touched down in twenty-three states, where Republicans hoped to gain or retain sixteen Senate seats and fourteen governorships. Not to mention retaining the party's majority in the House of Representatives. Hence our question: how far, if at all, did Trump's presence help in tipping the scales for his party? Agreed, there's no scientific way to tie effects to a single cause. Still, we can record what happened after the president's interventions.

- The Republicans' chief 2018 accomplishment was to retain control of the Senate. They did this by taking seats from Democrats in four states: Florida, Indiana, Missouri, and North Dakota. Hence a question: How much, if at all, were those shifts due to the eleven rallies that Trump held in those states?
- As it happened, he also made eleven visits to four other competitive states: Montana, West Virginia, Arizona, and Nevada. But despite the president's intercessions, Democrats retained the first two, and wrested the others from Republicans. Indeed, it could be argued that his appearances boomeranged, by moving Democrats to vote.
- Trump had seven rallies in five states where Republican governors were vulnerable: Illinois, Kansas, Michigan, Nevada, and Wisconsin. Democratic opponents flipped all five.
- Altogether, he intervened in thirty-one statewide contests. Republicans won fourteen of them, and Democrats carried seventeen. From another angle, Republicans flipped four seats while Democrats seized seven. Trump made a total of fifteen trips to Minnesota, Montana, Nevada, Pennsylvania, and West Virginia. In none of them did Republicans win the state.
- Republicans lost forty-two House seats in 2018. Twenty of them were in states Trump visited, and twenty-two where he didn't. Despite his three rallies in Pennsylvania, Republicans lost four of their thirteen districts. In Florida, Minnesota, Iowa, Illinois, and Michigan, where he also campaigned, ten seats also turned.
- Indeed, over a third of the House flips—sixteen seats in all—were in four states that he openly eschewed: California, New York, New Jersey, and Virginia. While they are largely blue turf, they contain red enclaves, some of which have long won House seats. If they were vulnerable in 2018, they weren't scheduled for the tour. The reason is obvious: the president prefers audiences where he can count on the cheers.

Measured by popular votes and offices that changed hands, the 2018 midterms had to count as a Democratic success. In all, Trump's efforts coincided with four Republican statewide wins. But in seven other states on his tour, his party's entrants lost.

What's worth adding is that that the Democrats didn't attempt to mount a counterpart of Trump's tour. The party had prominent figures such as Barack Obama and Hillary Clinton who could have appeared before cheering throngs. It's not as if they were shyly waiting to be asked. It wouldn't have hurt to fly to Florida, North Dakota, Missouri, and Indiana, which is where their party lost the Senate.

True, Trump's kind of demagoguery is not the Democrats' style. But Obama's 2008 campaign proved that mass events were both feasible and helpful. Hillary Clinton apparently felt that things were on track without them. Would that be wise for 2020?

That the Senate remained a GOP stronghold had to be disturbing. (One result: Justice Brett Kavanaugh.) So those four Democratic defeats warrant a postmortem, if only to see if there are lessons for 2020, when that chamber will again be on the ballots. The first fact was that the four losers—Bill Nelson, Joe Donnelly, Claire McCaskill, and Heidi Heitkamp—had carried their states six years earlier in 2012. True, Barack Obama, who did well nationally, headed their slates. Yet, beguilingly, he lost decisively in three of the states. He ended up ten points behind in Indiana and Missouri, and by nineteen points in North Dakota. In Florida, he barely slipped in by 74,309 votes of the 8,474,179 that were cast, a fraction of 1 percentage point.

So all four essentially got to the Senate on their own. Bill Nelson had the good fortune to draw a scapegrace opponent, Connie Mack, whose history of bar fights and divorce defaults put off even confirmed Republicans. Nelson won by thirteen points. Joe Donnelly in Indiana and Claire McCaskill of Missouri had similar luck. While campaigning, their opponents made expected attacks on abortion, but then followed them with these remarks on sexual assault: "Even when life begins in that horrible situation of rape, that is something that God intended to happen" and "If it's a legitimate rape, the female body has ways to try to shut the whole thing down."

Many observers felt this was why Donnelly won by six points and McCaskill by sixteen.

While in 2012, Obama got only 39 percent of the total in North Dakota, Heidi Heitkamp managed to come in 2,881 ahead in the 321,144 cast in the race, just under 1 percent. There was a time when her state was safe for Democrats. Quentin Burdick and Kent Conrad served in the Senate from 1960 through 2013. But that era seems at an end. Even Heitkamp's support for pipelines and disapproval of deficits weren't enough for reelection.

If Nelson's loss in Florida was perturbing for Democrats, 2018's other statewide race was promising. Their party's mayor of Tallahassee, Andrew Gillum, came within 32,464 votes—of 8,220,561—in the race for governor. And he came that close despite conducting an openly liberal campaign, the kind Republicans like to tag as socialist. Not to mention that Gillum was African American, in a state where 85 percent of the residents have other ancestries.

In much of the country, the majority of white voters make Republicans their party of choice, and that has long been so in Florida. Yet CNN's exit poll for the state found that 39 percent of all white voters went for Gillum, rising to 47 percent of white women, and further to 57 percent for white women with college degrees. These ratios—especially intertwined with gender and education—suggest that the GOP can't count on its dominant race as assuredly as it once did.

If Missouri, Indiana, and North Dakota are well settled in the Republican column, Democrats in these states do not lack for fortitude. Here's one indicator. The percentages in the table depict the votes cast for Donnelly, McCaskill, and Heitkamp, set against their states' totals for Hillary Clinton in 2016. As can be seen, the Democrats' rates in the 2018 midterms equaled or exceeded those for president.

SHOWING UP FOR THE SENATE		
2018 Turnouts in relation to 2016		
Democrats		Republicans
99%	Indiana	74%
105%	Missouri	79%
154%	North Dakota	83%

When citizens show up in such numbers, even though they know they're likely to lose, that expresses a depth of commitment. Heitkamp's followers were clearly there in force. Apparently, Republicans were so sure they would win that more of them stayed at home. That kind of complacency may take a toll in 2020.

11
ELECTORS: WHEN THEY SUPERSEDE

The closing hours of November 8, 2016, found jaws agape in millions of living rooms and local watering holes. Democrats and Republicans alike were stunned to learn that Donald J. Trump would be the nation's next president. True, given a large and varied nation, we cannot sense how the rest of the country might be tilting. Sadly, polls are about all we have; and every reputable sounding had forecast a sweep by Hillary Clinton.

Equally confounding was that Trump would enter the Oval Office despite having ended with 2,868,509 fewer votes. At that moment, even honors students began trying to recall how the Electoral College actually operates. (Like, who are its members, and do they assemble at a single location?)

In the great majority of cases, the candidate with the most popular votes glides into the White House. In particular, of fifty-four of the fifty-eight elections between 1788 and 2016, the electors simply affirmed the public tally. That's 93 percent.

The system, as installed in 1791 and amended in 1804, can still supersede the majority's will. Currently, the country is being governed by one of the four outliers.

As we all know, there was a foretaste in 2000. George W. Bush managed a single-digit edge in the Electoral College, despite drawing 530,893 fewer votes than Albert Gore. Its abiding impact was a full-scale Iraq incursion, which detonated an entire region, with no end in sight. It seems a safe surmise that had the popular tally prevailed, today's Middle East would be a far less embattled place.

Another consequence of 2000 was that the Supreme Court of the day, at that time an unabashed Republican redoubt, swiftly assumed jurisdiction. Indeed, its five Republican members were well aware that ambiguous ballots ("hanging chads") were still under recount in Florida. Without a trice of hesitation or reflection, the party's justices promptly gave the presidency to their slate's nominee. Showing a trace of chagrin, they counseled that their *Bush v. Gore* decision should not be recorded as a precedent.

The table below summarizes the statistics and scenarios of the occasions when second-count contenders were certified. The first noteworthy fact is that in all four of the years—1876, 1888, 2000, 2016—it was Republicans who got the nod. It's worth inquiring if something in the system induces this bias.

The Electoral College is a cousin of the Senate, in that states get two extra seats regardless of their size. This emerges most graphically among those allocated only one at-large seat in the House of Representatives. Thus Wyoming, Vermont, and other small states are accorded three electoral votes, which automatically triples their power in the presidential stakes. And true, this helps Republicans, to a point. Of the eight with only one House member, five were Republican (Alaska, Montana, Wyoming, both Dakotas) and three were Democratic (Vermont, Delaware, District of Columbia). At that level, Republicans at best get four extra Electoral College votes.[1]

2016		
65,853,625 (48.0%)	Hillary Clinton (D)	227 (42.2%)
62,985,106 (45.9%)	Donald Trump (R)	304 (56.5%)
2000		
51,009,810 (48.4%)	Albert Gore (D)	266 (49.4%)
50,642,412 (47.9%)	George Bush (R)	271 (50.4%)
1888		
5,534,488 (48.6%)	Grover Cleveland (D)	168 (41.9%)
5,443,892 (47.8%)	Benjamin Harrison (R)	233 (58.1%)
1876		
4,288,546 (50.9%)	Samuel Tilden (D)	184 (49.1%)
4,034,311 (47.9%)	Rutherford Hayes (R)	185 (50.1%)

In 1876 and 2000, Rutherford Hayes and George Bush had tenuous electoral showings, so they needed bonus votes to get over the top. (Bush had fifty-eight of them to Gore's forty-four, because he carried more smaller states.)

However, Benjamin Harrison and Donald Trump, in 1888 and 2016, would have won even were the added votes not available. As Trump ceaselessly tweets, he shouldn't be called a minority president, since he drew seventy-seven more electors than his opponent. In fact, Harrison did even better. His edge of sixty-five electors was in a considerably smaller Electoral College.

Except for Nebraska and Maine, in forty-eight states and the District of Columbia, it only takes one ballot to swing an entire electoral slate to a candidate. While so miniscule an edge has never occurred, some have been close. For example, in 2016, the 2,279,543 Republican votes cast in Michigan gave Trump a 10,703 edge over Clinton, giving him all of the state's sixteen electoral votes.

Now let's glance at New Jersey, a somewhat smaller but generally comparable state. There the Democrats' 2,148,279 votes gave them a massive victory over a diminished GOP. The downside was that fully 546,344 of the Democrats' harvest weren't needed to carry the state. I'll be calling them *excess* or *surplus* votes. While it's always wise to have a safety margin, well over what's required is a misuse of resources. In a Democratic dream, some of their New Jersey surplus might have been shipped to Michigan, where their 10,703 shortfall lost them the state.

Nationally, more Democratic votes are clustered in states with high excess quotients. Of Clinton's popular tally, an outsized 11,702,190 were in the surplus category. It was why she ended with only twenty states and the District of Columbia, and their 227 electoral yield. Trump's excess was visibly smaller, at 8,357,672. This tells us that his supporters were more widely dispersed, and could carry competitive states, even if not by crushing margins. Hence he ended with thirty states in his column, and his 304 electoral win. It's not that he had a strategy staff that deployed his 62,692,411 adherents where they could do the most good. Rather, political demography and cartography combined to favor his party.

The story's not over. There's a lot to be learned from the previous presidential race. So let's start with the surplus vote situation in 2012. In fact, Barack Obama had 11,802,492 excess votes, almost identical to Hillary Clinton's. Across the aisle, Mitt Romney had 6,800,670, measurably under Donald Trump's. Thus in theory, more of Romney's votes were strategically spread. Why did Obama win and Clinton lose?

Obama's win was decisive, with the electors giving him 332 of their votes, fully 105 more than Hillary Clinton's 227. Nor was this due to Barack Obama's incumbency. That's not an automatic advantage. Ask Jimmy Carter, Herbert Hoover, and William Howard Taft.

So the question is how a Democrat can avoid the Electoral College trap. After all, Harry Truman, John Kennedy, Lyndon Johnson, and Jimmy Carter each did it, with Bill Clinton and Barack Obama managing it twice. Let's return to Obama in 2012 for his formula. We'll start with his popular total.

On paper, Obama got 65,752,017 votes in 2012, which seems almost identical with Clinton's 65,853,652. But if we attune their tallies to a growing electorate, we need to raise Obama's figure by 3.8 percent. For our purposes, an equivalent count for him becomes 67,724,458.

What we've learned is that Clinton's count was actually 2,147,288 behind Obama's. That's not a small number. (Trump was only 286,763 below Romney.) Had Clinton managed to match Obama's 2012 count, that popular total would have given her an easy win via the Electoral College.

Here's how and why. True, the added 2,527,838 for the Democrats would be spread across the nation. Even so, that total would have included more than enough leverage to shift the outcomes in Wisconsin, Michigan, and Pennsylvania, which Trump carried by only 77,744. Indeed, such an infusion might have brought her Ohio, Iowa, and Florida as well. After all, Obama won them.

So the lesson is straightforward. If Democrats are to avoid the Electoral College snare, they must assemble an outsized popular tally.[2] All those surplus votes in safe states may provide a warm feeling. But the presidency can only be won nationally, which requires building battalions in equivocal terrain. It's what Obama did, and why he won. Think Florida and Iowa. It's how 2018 saw local Democrats turning seats in Kansas, Oklahoma, and South Carolina. The message for 2020 should be obvious. Democrats won't win the White House via California, even with its huge electoral total. It will only happen by mobilizing in states that the party too often views as inhospitable terrain.

HOW REPRESENTATIVE IS THE HOUSE?

Imagine that each party's number of seats in the House of Representatives matched the share of votes its candidates received. Republicans running in Illinois received 39 percent of the votes in the state's eighteen House races. A close matching would give them seven of the eighteen seats, which is just about 39 percent.

Had this formula been used for the House that is currently sitting, Democrats would have 259 members, or twenty-four more than the 235 they now have.

The main reason was cynical gerrymandering by GOP state legislatures. Among their shortfalls were five seats in Texas, three in North Carolina and Ohio, and two in Indiana.[1] Due to shameless mapmaking, Wisconsin Republicans were able to turn 46 percent of the votes into 62 percent of the state's delegation. The only Democratic counterpart was Maryland, which yielded them two extra seats.

But there's more. Despite their losses from contorted districts, Democrats won 53 percent of all House votes nationally and ended up with 54 percent of the membership. That seems a pretty equitable result.

Or take another measure. A basic stratagem in drawing district lines for partisan advantage is to force the other party to "waste" its votes. That's what happened in notoriously gerrymandered North Carolina, where Democrats expended 544,235 votes on each seat they won and Republicans got theirs with 189,644 apiece.

Yet nationally, Democrats averaged 255,197 votes per seat, almost identical to the Republicans' 253,994. I can't think of another year when the two sides were as close by that yardstick.

So it would seem that in the current House, neither party is losing. Here's the reason: Republicans fared almost as badly in heavily Democratic states as

Democrats did in Republican-dominated ones when it comes to comparing seat allocation to statewide vote totals. In bright-blue states, the GOP got twenty-one fewer places than their votes warranted. Notably, they were two down in New York and Illinois, three down in New Jersey, and a dazzling ten down in California.[2]

How this occurred differed from the manipulations faced by Democrats. California's congressional districts are crafted by an independent panel. In New Jersey, New York, and Illinois, the districts that Democrats won in 2018 had previously gone to Republicans. If that could happen, it should be a sign of nonpartisan mapping.

So what brought about the GOP's underrepresentation? As was pointed out earlier, Republicans chose to sit out thirty-nine races in 2018, whereas Democrats skipped only three. I estimate that these blanks caused a dip of 2,473,998 votes cast for Republican House candidates.

Another reason is more recondite. In 2018, Democrats increased their victory margin in some fairly competitive states, notably by doing well in reddish suburbs. In the dozen states where Democrats had their best tallies, they carried an arresting 125 of the 148 districts. In Connecticut and Massachusetts, they took every one. Yet these states also had sizable pools of Republicans—in fact, 11,801,177 in the states together—who came away with only twenty-three House successes.

GOP supporters in these states sank 629,842 of their votes into each of their seats, while Democrats got theirs for 175,936. Few gerrymander templates attain that ratio. In California alone, Republicans ended up with only seven of the fifty-three places in their state's delegation. Geared to votes, they would have had ten more.

Much is said about how Democrats coalesce in urban areas, where their votes are clustered in overlarge majorities. It appears that Republicans are also assembling with fellow thinkers, even if the milieus can't be as readily identified as a Phoenix or a Philadelphia. As a result, Democrats have felt less need to manipulate maps. (As I've noted, only Maryland is truly culpable on this score.)

As matters now stand, there's no partisan consistency to the relationship between votes and seats. It comes close to pure equality in Republican Florida and Democratic Colorado. It's most divergent in Democratic New Jersey and Republican Kentucky.

Of course, nonpartisan maps are possible. Pennsylvania's, which was imposed in 2018 by its highest court, is an excellent model. But it's unclear how even a fair-minded map would aid California's Republicans, apart from adopting multimember districts and preferential ballots. The Supreme Court's Republican majority has now decreed that it is not the province of federal judges to umpire cartographic quarrels. (At least that's how they put it. Their party's stockpile of extra seats was under attack.)[3]

So does the current composition of the House mirror the electorate's will? In an odd way, it does. Each party's deficits in states are redressed elsewhere. It's almost as if Arkansas's bypassed Democrats gain a voice via Rhode Island. Still, state by state, representation is woefully out of kilter. In thirty-one states, district maps help one party, albeit not always by conscious design. That the parties' averages turn out to be similar should not deter moves for nonpartisan commissions and a commitment to fairness.

HOW SKEWED IS THE SENATE?

Republicans have held the Senate's majority for eighteen of the last twenty-six years, leaving only six for Democrats and two when there was a tie. This disparity is likely to continue. Or will so long as Republicans can count on smaller states, with their two seats, regardless of population.[1]

As we are constantly reminded, California's 39,747,267 residents and Wyoming's 585,501 both get two senators. This gives Laramie householders sixty-seven times more say in the Senate than those in Santa Rosa.

The Senate wasn't meant to represent actual people. The framers made clear it was there to safeguard the states, on the premise they all had equal status. Since its structure is embedded in Article I, there's little chance it will be changed. One recourse is to spell out how far that chamber departs from a popular template.

Due to an interplay of ideology, history, and happenstance, Republicans tend to do better in less settled and more rural states. So the twenty-five smallest states command half the chamber's seats, despite having only 17 percent of the nation's population. And in this smaller half, twenty-nine are Republicans against twenty-one Democrats. That eight-seat edge can be decisive on Senate roll calls. Viewed the other way, the twenty-five largest states, which house 83 percent of Americans, have a closer ratio of twenty-six Democrats and twenty-four Republicans. In a word, the two-seats system doesn't give the Democrats a comparable bonus.

As was noted, Republicans have had three times the odds of ending with most of the Senate's seats, which means that they are more likely to prevail when rolls are called. Hence this question: when Republicans win on the floor, how many people out in the country are behind those tallies?

In fact, there's no settled way of calibrating the Senate's human constituencies. As was seen in the previous chapter, parsing the House of Representatives is easy. In November 2018, Democratic candidates won 54 percent of the major parties' votes. Even with contorted maps and suppressive schemes, their party ended with 54 percent of the seats. A perfect fit.

Deconstructing the Senate is harder. One approach might be to assign each senator half of his or her state's population. Since Ohio has a Democrat and a Republican, both would be seen as having a half-state base of 5,859,284. A problem is that this figure includes everyone inside Ohio's borders, even babies and noncitizens. It also includes everyone who voted against these two incumbents.

Another method is to find how many votes each of them received. Ohio's Rob Portman won reelection in 2016 with 3,118,567, while Sherrod Brown kept his seat in 2018 with 2,355,923. Does this mean that Portman has more of a mandate? Perhaps. But his higher figure was less a testament to him than because he ran in a presidential year, when turnouts are always higher. Also, there are 1,996,908 Democrats who turned out in 2016 and 2,053,963 Republicans who did in 2018, but who aren't counted because they voted for the losing candidates. Are senators supposed to represent only the victors?

The best, albeit imperfect, way is to add up the votes cast on each party's line in all the relevant Senate elections. After all, citizens who voted for losing candidates also wanted to record how they felt. So as the current Senate has one hundred members, we'll include all votes for all two hundred contenders for those seats.

(Independents like Bernie Sanders are counted as Democrats because they caucus with that party. Other minor parties are not included in the totals because none of their candidates have ever won a Senate seat.)

Here's a number you are unlikely to have seen, since as far as I know, it hasn't been compiled before: 218,552,126. It is how many ballots were cast in three cycles—2014, 2016, 2018—in the contests that decided the current makeup of the Senate. The total divides into 121,971,401 (or 56 percent) for the Democrats, and 96,580,725 (or 44 percent) for Republicans. One bottom line is that the Republicans obtained their current majority of fifty-three seats with a minority 44 percent of the votes cast in Senate contests. Here is how these ratios played out when important chips were down.

- In April 2017, the Senate confirmed Neil Gorsuch by a fifty-four-vote majority, from fifty-one Republicans and three Democrats. (One

Republican didn't vote.) The fifty-four senators who elevated Gorsuch represented 46 percent of the electorate that gave them their seats.

- In December 2017, the Senate rushed through a regressive tax bill with fifty-one Republican votes. (One opposed it.) Those fifty-one represented 45 percent of the voting public.
- In October 2017, the Senate confirmed Brett Kavanaugh by a 50–48 margin. That majority had forty-nine Republicans and one Democrat, with two Republicans not voting. The fifty who anointed Kavanaugh represented 46 percent of the active electorate.

For the record, opposition to both Gorsuch and Kavanaugh came in at 54 percent, measured by the vote-base of senators who contested their confirmations. By the same gauge, 55 percent of voting Americans disapproved of the tax bill.

Nor is this an anomaly. I've added votes-to-seats quotients for all twelve Senates, going back to 1994. Altogether, there were some four hundred races, including special elections, as when Al Franken was replaced.

As the table below shows, in four of the twelve years (2000, 2002, 2006, 2010), seats won basically paralleled the electoral results. Among the other eight, Republicans had more seats than their votes would warrant—I call this "overage"—in six of the sessions, leaving Democrats just one. (I'll be returning to that one.)

Moreover, the overage has grown very visibly in the three most recent Senates, notwithstanding the Democrats' popular sweep in 2018.

In sum, Article I favors Republicans. Since they carry more smaller states, they win their pairs of seats with fewer votes. Even when Democrats take 53 percent of the Senate's popular count, they cannot control the chamber.

As matters stand, the only recourse for Democrats is a presidential triumph. The best model was 2008. (Prior to that, one must go back to 1964.) In Barack Obama's first bid, he routed John McCain by 9,550,176 votes, three times Hillary Clinton's edge.

His coattails helped Democrats win Senate seats in purple states like Colorado and North Carolina, in both cases by a comfortable 53 percent. More striking were Senate victories in South Dakota (62 percent), West Virginia (64 percent), Iowa (68 percent), Montana (73 percent), even Arkansas (80 percent). The party began 2009 with fifty-nine Senate seats. It had much the same margin in the House of Representatives.

VOTES WON VS/ SEATS WON			
Ratios for Republican Senate Candidates			
Votes	Year	Seats	Overage
49%	1994	52	+3
50%	1996	55	+5
51%	2000	50	0
50%	2002	51	+1
49%	2004	53	+4
48%	2006	48	0
46%	2008	41	-5
48%	2010	47	-1
47%	2012	45	-2
49%	2014	54	+5
46%	2016	52	+6
44%	2018	53	+7
48%	Average	50	+2

As it happens, the states that had Senate contests in 2008 will be up again in 2020. This time, though, the focus is on Republican incumbents. At least four of them will have to be defeated if Democrats are to control both chambers on Capitol Hill. The final table in this chapter lists six states that belong in the competitive column. Here, as in earlier analyses, the emphasis will be on party commitment, gauged by off-year turnouts. As can be seen, Democrats were more likely to take the time and trouble in all six of the states, with their readiness well ahead in four of them.

COMPETITIVE SENATE STATES		
2018 Turnouts Relative to 2016		
Democrats		Republicans
96%	Maine	75%
102%	Iowa	76%
60%	Colorado	43%
102%	Arizona	91%
97%	Georgia	95%
75%	North Carolina	72%

FIVE—FOUR JUSTICE

IS IT PRINCIPLE OR PARTY?

A tacit agreement prevails about the Supreme Court. The accepted designations for its members are denoted as *liberals* or *conservatives*.

This chapter will propose that this usage is misleading, and obstructs understanding of how the judiciary exerts its authority. For example, there's nothing "conservative" about championing the ownership of assault weapons. It's a major Republican plank.

True, federal judges do not face public elections, let alone on party slates. But in recent years, partisan allegiances have been openly voiced in the choice and confirmation of judicial candidates. Republicans have been especially steadfast about elevating only their own kind to federal benches. Its faithful affiliate, the Federalist Society, serves as its screening committee.

Throughout this chapter, the Court's members will be associated with the parties whose agendas they embrace.

Since Dwight Eisenhower's inauguration in 1953, altogether twenty-seven justices have served on the Supreme Court. Nineteen were nominated by Republican presidents, leaving only eight who were nominated by Democrats. This was due largely to the GOP's holding the presidency for forty of those years, as opposed to twenty-eight for the Democrats. Another factor was that more vacancies, to death or retirement, fell during Republican administrations.

The last time a Democratic president chose a chief justice was almost three-quarters of a century ago, in 1946, when Harry Truman appointed Fred Vinson. All four of his successors have been Republican choices. The last year Democratic appointments held a five-to-four majority was in 1953, the opening year of Eisenhower's presidency. During his tenure, he named five justices, installing the Republican dominance that continues to this day.

For at least a generation, the court was not palpably partisan. *Brown v. Board of Education*, the historic desegregation case, was decided unanimously, under the leadership of Chief Justice Earl Warren. The vote on the now-contentious *Roe v. Wade* was 7–2, crossing conventional lineups. Adhering to Warren's paradigm, GOP appointments like David Souter, William Brennan, and John Paul Stevens eschewed partisan ties. Sandra Day O'Connor and Anthony Kennedy had bursts of independence, but they joined in finding ways to give the 2000 election to the younger George Bush. Chief Justice William Rehnquist, who was elevated by Ronald Reagan, wore his party colors openly, but he was often outvoted, a hapless turn for the head of the court.

Today's court is more sharply split than any since the 1930s, with a 5–4 bifurcation, as if etched in stone. Nor has this been by happenstance. On the contrary, it has been a long-standing Republican strategy. For almost three decades, since Clarence Thomas took his seat in 1991, justices named by Republican presidents have wholly understood why they were chosen. Simply stated, it was to embed their party's platforms and policies in the life of the nation through selective readings of statutes and constitutional provisions.

When people hold power, and inevitably some do, it should have some validation. The best way, as we heard in Political Science 101, is to get the most votes. (Hence much mulling about the Electoral College and the allocation of senators.)

If we wanted to pick the ten most powerful individuals in today's United States, it could be argued that five of them are the majority members of the Supreme Court. Hence a simple question. Why should they have that sway? It's not as if they were personally elected and must face voters at the end of a term. (Top judges in seven states do get there via the ballot box.)[1] True, they were chosen by elected presidents and confirmed by elected senators. But justices keep their seats long after those who named and approved them are gone.

So it might seem rational to conclude that five individuals who were chosen and remain at several removes from public scrutiny would use their powers sparingly. Especially that they hold their command by a single vote. Here's a sampling of how the five justices have attuned the nation to accord with Republican parameters.

- The close of 2000 Election Day found Florida with only 537 votes between the two major candidates out of 5,963,110 that were cast. Given that microscopic margin, the states' judges agreed that a manual recount was needed. The Supreme Court's five Republicans intervened to overrule the state, which led to installing Bush as a minority president. (*Bush v. Gore, 2000*)

- In 2007, Lilly Ledbetter sued her employer, a global conglomerate, contending that her lower pay was due to sex discrimination. Republicans have long sympathized with employers, who find such claims unseemly and a drain on profits. By rereading a "paycheck accrual rule," five Republicans rejected Ledbetter's plea, conveying to other workers that they needn't file, either. (*Ledbetter v. Goodyear Tire & Rubber, 2007*)

- A year later, five Republicans annulled a District of Columbia ordinance that had hoped to reduce firearms accidents. To do so, they reread the word "militia" in the Second Amendment, which had hitherto been given a military meaning. Thus the five created a shield for gun owners, a prime Republican constituency. (*District of Columbia v. Heller, 2008*)

- In 2010, five Republicans again came to the aid of corporations, this time allowing them to finance candidates and elections. Their rationale was that the First Amendment ensured "speech" of business entities. (*Citizens United v. Federal Election Commission, 2010*)

- In 2013, five Republicans ruled that a 1965 voting rights act was unconstitutional because it gave federal officials undue power over state agencies. The states the five chose to protect were mainly Southern, Republican, and committed to maintaining the dominance of white voters. (*Shelby County v. Holder, 2013*)

- With the 2016 advent of a Republican administration, its five judicial allies were soon asked to uphold some of its provocative actions. Hence a 2018 decision expanding its power to imprison immigrants. Another approved the banning of petitioners from entire countries. (*Nielsen v. Preap, 2019; Trump v. Hawaii, 2018*)

- In a traditional Republican vein, the five joined in their party's campaign to eviscerate labor unions. Under some contracts, all workers had to pay dues, since they shared in benefits. The five held in 2018 that "free speech rights" of nonmembers relieved them of that obligation. (*Janus v. American Federation of State, 2018* exempted *Federation of State, County, and Municipal Employees*)

- In Ohio, Republicans sought to reinforce their dominance. They singled out citizens who had missed some recent elections, knowing that most of them usually voted Democratic. A nondescript card was sent out, made to look like junk mail. Those who didn't reply, and most didn't, were not allowed to vote when they next showed up. The Republican five readily approved Ohio's stratagem, also in 2018. (*Husted v. A. Philip Randolph Institute, 2018*)

• More than a few legislatures, most in Republican hands, created districts that gave their party more seats than their votes would warrant. A 2019 case asked the Court to require more equitable maps. The five declined to intervene, contending that "partisan gerrymandering claims present political questions beyond the reach of the federal courts."[2] Hence the perpetuation of Republican rule, even when there is majority opposition. (*Rucho v. Common Cause, 2019*)

At this time of writing, four of the five show little inclination, often none at all, to temper the sweep of their decisions. After all, that's why Article III awarded them lifetime tenure. But the four also seem to feel that the general public will regard them as impartial solons, and hence exempt from public censure. It was this ascription of legitimacy that saw earlier courts through the contentious *Brown* and *Roe* decisions. One difference is that neither of these was 5–4. The first was bipartisan and unanimous; the second was a predominantly Republican 7–2.

Past a certain point, self-possession can segue into arrogance. This happened eight decades ago, when an earlier Republican court continued to nullify policies and programs supported by Democratic majorities. A proposal was floated to add more personnel to the panel, which Congress can legally do. It never came to the floor. But the message was heard, and the "Nine Old Men," as they were then called, began to rein themselves in.

If the five keep on as they have, one eventuality seems sure. We will see poll questions submitted to the public, asking for reactions to court decisions. Some might run:

Do you agree that five men in Washington should be able to tell all women in the country that they must give birth whenever they become pregnant?

Do you agree that five men in Washington, DC, should be able to decree that homosexual men and women may be fired from their jobs?

While open scrutiny like this has always been accepted for the executive and legislative branches, thus far the judiciary has been protected from political reproach. That's thus far. But past a certain point, Democrats will no longer sit silently, if five life-tenured Republicans seem bent on reshaping the nation.

Chief Justice Roberts is plainly worried lest something like this happen. His tactic has been to reduce the number of 5–4 Republican decisions. This done, his thinking seems to run, those that remain won't seem so egregious. Thus in 2012, he joined with the four Democrats to preserve the Obama health-care law. (His fellow Republicans showed no hesitancy annulling it, even though it had passed the Senate by a 60–39 vote.)

Early in 2019, Roberts sided with the Democrats again to stop Louisiana from closing the state's last remaining abortion clinic, even though such shut-tering is a high Republican priority. Later in 2019, he once more joined the Democratic bloc to scotch a Republican scheme that would skew the census to undercount citizens who tend to vote Democratic.

As this book goes to press, the Court has agreed to take several cases that involve strong Republican positions. One is to allow the current administration to nullify Barack Obama's program on Deferred Action for Childhood Arrivals. Another will permit the present Environmental Protection Agency to invalidate California's rules on automotive emissions. A third would let the current president keep his tax records secret.

It's safe to assume that the five Republicans know how they'd like to vote on these and similar cases. Their predispositions are patent, and it's why they were chosen for the court. So it will be revealing to see if some of them hedge. If they don't, we can expect the Supreme Court itself to become an open target. This will put Republicans on the defensive, since it's their votes that have given the branch a partisan cast.

15

TWO TOWN HALLS

Imagine a party meeting where one hundred people are present. Scanning the room, you find two individuals of African origin, plus ten with Hispanic or Asian antecedents. All the remaining eighty-eight are white. It would be a typical Republican gathering, derived from CNN polls during the 2018 mid-term election. As it happened, there was a similar distribution at the GOP's 2016 convention.

This chapter will use this trope to portray the social makeup of the two parties. So let's go across town to a Democratic meeting. There we find that only sixty of the one hundred claim European ancestries. Another nineteen are black, fourteen are Hispanic, and seven have other origins. This puts their white-to-other ratio at a relatively close 3:2, compared with the Republicans' more pronounced 1:7.

We can presume that both parties, on the whole, like their current compositions. Insofar as that is so, white Republicans feel most comfortable with people of their lineage, and would prefer that others remain at the margins. True, two of their presidential aspirants have Cuban parents. Still, their policies and platforms cannot be distinguished from those of white co-partisans.

White Democrats like being in a varied party. They were particularly pleased to have Barack Obama as their president. Indeed, they look forward to the nation having more racial diversity, as would occur with expanded immigration. As will be considered in a later chapter, being identified as white carries less weight with Democrats than is the case with Republicans.

A Republican assemblage would have fifty-five men and forty-five women, a visible but not an egregious disproportion. Most of the women are married, almost wholly to Republican husbands. As it happens, the Democrats' ratio is fifty-eight women to forty-two men, a sixteen-point gulf. It's hard to think of another general association where women so outnumber men. Democratic men are aware that they stand less chance when impending candidacies open up. Still, they prefer a cosexual party, even if they have a more muted role.

Suppose that the parties decided to have events for only their unmarried members. From a Republican one-hundred-person pool, the singles contingent would number thirty-four, with eighteen men and sixteen women, a fairly even match. The Democratic scene is quite different. Out of its pool of one hundred people, fully forty-seven would be unmarried, not far from half. Moreover, that group would have eighteen men and twenty-nine women, close to a 40–60

Democrats	PARTY PROFILES: 2018	Republicans
	Gender	
42%	Men	55%
58%	Women	45%
	Income	
29%	Over $100,000	38%
28%	$50,000–$100,00	30%
43%	Under $50,000	32%
$71,176	Median	$82,857
	Education	
21%	Advanced Degree	13%
25%	Bachelor's	23%
54%	Non-BA	64%
	Race	
54%	White	88%
18%	Black	2%
14%	Hispanic	7%
9%	Other	3%
	Age	
24%	65 & Older	29%
36%	45–64	43%
24%	30–44	19%
16%	Under 30	9%
50	Median	55

ratio. If the Democrats are much more a women's party, single women lift the equation even higher. One issue come to the fore. Single women are more likely to think about the availability of abortion, especially with longer spans before marriage, if it occurs at all. This doubtless veers them toward the Democratic side. Indeed, married women haven't forgotten their single days, plus a possibility that they might be on their own again.

The parties diverge in their income distributions, but not markedly. While the Democrats have a more pronounced bottom tier, the Republicans are closer to a pillar or column. There is a 16 percent gap in the parties' median incomes, which can be seen as substantial or modest. What does emerge is that both parties are amalgams of classes, combining households that are quite comfortable with some on more tenuous margins. That noted, other figures on the table suggest why the parties' coalitions vary as much as they do.

One reason for the Democrats' lower median and larger bottom tier is that its supporters tend to be younger. Another is that a third of its adherents are Hispanic or black, who face fewer opportunities for higher-paid occupations. The Republicans present quite another picture. To start, their black and brown quotients are relatively low. Given that whites comprise 88 percent of the party, they must fill up much of its bottom income echelon. Simply stated, the Republicans now house more of the poorer white population than the Democrats. One factor was that making a bid for former Confederate states also gave them the poorest region in the country. (For the statistically inclined, states with high Republican turnouts correlate strongly with low median incomes.)

The parties' higher tiers are also diverse, although not as much as might first appear. The CNN table records that 29 percent of Democrats and 38 percent of Republicans have incomes of at least $100,000. That is correct. But what it doesn't factor in is that 2018 had 9,852,442 more Democrats casting ballots. With that clarified, the counts are 17,492,684 to 19,117,536, not a gaping divide.

So on measures of income, the parties seem quite similar. True, more Republicans are in the top tier, which is not surprising, given the party's focus on wealth and profits. Still, as the table shows, they form a graduated 38-30-32 column, rather than a rich-poor pyramid.

We know why affluent Republicans prefer their party. It is committed to reducing their taxes, so they will have more money for their own acquisitions and enjoyments. (The 2017 Tax Cuts Law affirmed that promise.) Moreover, they resent seeing their earnings passed to people they regard as less energetic than themselves.

Less easily explained are Democrats who live comfortably. Just on taxes, they support higher levies on themselves, to assist other citizens and social purposes. Seemingly, they are less drawn to the aforementioned acquisitions and enjoyments. And they appear to favor a less-stratified society, even to the extent that they will move down a notch or two. It's for another book to decipher possible interplays of guilt, compassion, and conscience. What's notable is that this stratum has grown too large to be dismissed as a small elite of intellectuals and entertainers. It is now carrying precincts in Kansas and Kentucky, making such states fair game for Democrats.

That Republicans are older is commonly known, and it helps to explain their higher incomes. What has kept the party going is that these stalwarts are steadier voters. They also remember when citizens of their stock were more numerous, not to say respected. Plus they have more free time to go to the polls. As can be seen, the Democrats do markedly better among citizens under the age of thirty. While most have political views, far fewer have gotten the voting habit. When one young citizen was told his state allowed him to vote by mail, he asked how to obtain a postage stamp. If Democrats increased their youthful voting by just a few percentage points, they could readily take command of the Senate. Republicans are well aware of this. Hence states they control have been taking steps to keep students from voting. For example, gun owners' photo identification cards are accepted, but those issued by public colleges are not.

On education, the most visible differences are at the high and low ends. A substantial twenty-one of one hundred Democrats have advanced degrees, versus thirteen for Republicans. But it's unlikely that most of these Democrats are physicians or attorneys, let alone MBAs. They're more apt to be in fields like teaching, social work, and public service, with relatively modest earnings.

A decade and a half ago, when John Kerry sought to unseat George Bush, college graduates were divided evenly between the two parties. By 2018, however, only 40 percent of bachelors' degree holders were voting for Republicans, leaving 60 percent supporting Democrats.

This migration of college graduates away from Republican ranks suggests that they have been estranged by the party's coarse demeanor and arrogant postures. They don't want to deny Darwin, claim that the climate isn't changing, or extol the death penalty. These and other GOP stances run counter to the tenor of most higher education.

True, not all graduates are intellectuals. Indeed, much of the Republican leadership has suitable credentials. The president enrolled at the University of Pennsylvania. (Even so, he had his lawyer threaten calamitous suits if it released his grades.) The party's current core on the Supreme Court—Clarence Thomas, Samuel Alito, Neil Gorsuch, and Brett Kavanaugh—all attended Ivy League law schools. Ted Cruz, who placed second in the primaries, went to Princeton. The incumbent attorney general is a Columbia alumnus, and the treasury secretary has a degree from Yale. All have agreed to provide a patrician veneer for a rambunctious administration.

16

A NEW ELECTORATE

Even before the January 2017 installation of the 45th president and the 115th Congress, a coherent opposition was taking shape. It didn't have a name or a program or consensus, or even agreement on what it was for. Rather, its adherents knew who and what they were against. They had a singular goal: to end the tenure of the president as soon as possible, along with those who had chosen to empower him.

In just two years, from 2016 to 2018, the Democratic share of the voting public increased from 48 percent to 53 percent. Such an upsurge in so short a span is extremely rare, and in national reckonings, five points is a significant swing. If nothing else, those who want to retain office ought to ask why, or at least try to ponder the public's mood. But there are no signs that the president or his party have done this. On the contrary, they feel they still have an ample mandate, and need only feed the spirits of their 2016 loyalists.

Clearly, this strategy didn't work in 2018, considering the loss of the House of Representatives, plus a passel of state legislatures and governorships.[1] Yet there's no sign that their 2020 campaign plan will be any different.

The GOP sees itself as a party of deep principles as well as pragmatic policies. At the forefront are its stances on abortion and firearms; the first with its irreversible view of human life, and the second celebrating instruments designed to end it.[2] There is also its antipathy to democracy, signaled by constricting eligibility for the franchise. Less overt but equally evident are anxieties over the increasing racial diversity, impelling restrictions on immigration and retreats from civil rights. Yet recent voting, poll responses, and social trends make clear that these and other GOP canons have become minority stances.

- All polls show ambivalence about abortion. Many people get uneasy about the procedure as pregnancies proceed. Still, of those with opinions—and almost all have—fully 73 percent of 2018 voters wished to preserve *Roe v. Wade*, which means they want the procedure to remain available.

- On guns, exit polls found 61 percent saying they wanted more controls than currently imposed.
- When asked if they viewed fraudulent voting or suppressive measures as a greater danger, 60 percent of people said they were more worried about attempts to reduce the rolls.
- An earlier poll, in 2016, found 74 percent saying they believed undocumented workers should be eligible for a legal status rather than deported. This response may be lower now, since the president has devoted much of his term to demonizing immigrants. Still, voting numbers suggest that a solid majority haven't changed their minds. Case in point: the total lack of impact when he consigned troops to the Rio Grande on the eve of 2018 voting.

Other samplings have found most Americans favoring serious steps about the climate, less reliance on incarceration, and more open views of sexuality and marriage.

At the same time, research shows that Democrats are less ideologically engaged. Alan Abramowitz of Emory University, a leading political scientist, has devised ways to quantify how deeply people feel. On his scale of ideas and issues, Republicans come out 82 percent more passionate than Democrats.

Thus the 2018 CNN poll found 66 percent of Republicans painting themselves as *conservatives*. (The interviews also gave them a *moderate* option, which most of them eschewed.) Across the aisle, only 46 percent of Democrats made *liberal* their choice. (There wasn't a *progressive* box.) Across the country, this would have self-styled conservatives surpassing liberals, 34,068,180 to 28,014,338. It's statistics like that which hearten the GOP.

If so many Democrats are diffident about ideology, it's because they see the liberal label as constricting, burdened with a checklist of beliefs. Current voters like to see themselves as independent spirits, with their own penchants and principles. In fact, it includes an aesthetic sensibility, which abhors Donald Trump's deportment as demeaning of the presidency. It dishonors an entire nation to have a schoolyard bully at its head.

In all, changes we're seeing are less outwardly political than in the internal sensibilities of actual individuals. Americans are becoming increasingly open in their thinking, as they adapt to social and global trends. Not least are new and exacting occupations and technologies, with the sophistication they expect.

The most revealing indicator is level of education. Each year finds more of the electorate earning additional years of schooling. (Our most recent figures found 1,956,032 bachelor's degrees awarded, totaling to about half the relevant age group.) Among all those voting in 2018, four of every ten possessed at least a four-year degree. What's striking is that 46 percent of Democrats were in this pool, while only 39 percent of Republicans were. For many, really most, having completed college is transformative, a decisive rite of passage, a route to becoming a different kind of person. Allow a longtime academic a few musings on this score.

High schools are basically local. Their mission is to serve communities, with almost all their pupils living nearby. Those who end their education at that tier tend to bring more bounded outlooks into their adult lives.

Colleges, even those with regional enrollments, open students to wider realms. This involves a lot more than the topics taught in classrooms. Students know they are preparing themselves for new spheres of knowledge, employment, and citizenship. And that also entails new approaches to the scope and substance of politics.

It's a fact that most professors are liberal, if not overtly Democratic. So is the ambience of many campuses. That noted, it isn't clear how far this bias leaves a lasting imprint on undergraduates. After all, college life is an interlude. The real world starts after graduation.

Still, most of what is experienced during campus years is not explicitly ideological. Advanced instruction does not allow abbreviated answers. College students are expected to elaborate. Whether the subject is urban sociology, fashion merchandising, or software engineering, syllabi stress understanding complexities and coping with contradictions. Students learn to write and think in paragraphs.

This helps to explain the link between additional years in classrooms and Democratic voting. True, Democrats do devise mantras. "Medicare for All" and "Free Tuition" are recent examples But once pronounced, they feel obliged to spell out every codicil, including actuarial projections and cost-benefit ratios. Or proposals on climate change will be supplemented with software spreadsheets and mathematical models. Republicans believe that gripping phrases suffice. No need was felt to accompany "Build the Wall!" with a budget for its 1,954 miles.

Such shortcutting has given the GOP its populist veneer. Most conspicuous have been Donald Trump's rallies, which he began during the 2016 primaries and made a hallmark of his presidency. They've worked because of their avid audiences, willing to roar back on cue. It's hard to visualize an assemblage of Democrats thundering "Lock Her Up!" or "Send Them Back!"

To be sure, Barack Obama attracted upward of 80,000 admirers at Denver's Empower Field at Mile High and 240,000 in Chicago's Grant Park. They didn't lack for fervor. But there was no rancor or venom. Perhaps there will always be an appetite for red meat. But each year sees its avatars outnumbered by voters who prefer a more urbane diet.

Also in the mix is the ubiquity of livelihoods that call for conversational skills. Nor does this hold only with well-paid professions. In hosts of occupations, an expected skill is the ability to *explain*, whether how a new device operates or the provenance of items on a menu. Here, too, Democrats, in their positions or as a party, appeal to people accustomed to thinking and reading and listening.

Today, the divide is less between blue and white collars than a willingness to adjust to the century ahead, anticipate a transformed future, and refurbish yourself to meet it. Not surprisingly, milieus like Seattle and Silicon Valley, Route 128 and the Beltway, are heavily Democratic. In fact, replicas of them can now be found all across the country: Witness 2018 outcomes in Oklahoma, Iowa, and Kansas.

Also relevant is that, at last count, fully 57 percent of bachelor's degrees and 58 percent of advanced degrees were earned by women. More than coincidentally, in the 2018 midterms, 59 percent of the women who voted backed Democratic candidates.

To be sure, 36 percent of Republicans boast at least one diploma. But that should not occasion surprise. The most common bachelor's and master's degrees are in business, with 561,851 annual awards. Engineering also ranks high, at 189,036; with law enforcement, at 71,118, a popular major. For a considerable catchment of students, the highlights of higher education are football weekends and fraternity parties. How or why this correlates with party choice deserves some research.

17
A PARTISAN PRESIDENT

Here's a question for the waning hours of November 3, once it is settled that Donald Trump will be packing his bags. To what degree was he evicted because he was the person he was? (Among other things, a blustering bully.) And to what extent was it due to his heading a fervid Republican administration, which was buttressed by party loyalists in its legislative and judicial branches?

The past three and some years have belonged to Donald Trump. His presence has suffused the nation, even more than his most honored predecessors. A piece of evidence: Starting in January 2017, his name has been on every single front page of the *New York Times*. So I turned to May 1936, when Franklin Roosevelt was nearing the end of his historic first term. Yet I found that during its thirty-one days, the *Times'* first page headlined him on only thirteen of them ("President Rejects PWA Earmarking," "President Plans Trip to Southwest").

Our forty-fifth commander-in-chief didn't gain and maintain his dominance solely on his own. There had to be interests and individuals willing to sustain and support his vendettas. The chief of these has been the Republican Party.

As is widely known, Trump first registered politically in 1987, at the age of forty-one, when he put himself down as a Republican.[1] He switched to the Democrats in 2001 and stayed with them until 2009. After several shifts in allegiance, he signed on with the GOP again in 2012. Within five years, he was being sworn in to be that party's nineteenth president.

It was not unprecedented for Republicans to co-opt outsiders. Abraham Lincoln picked a Democrat, Andrew Johnson, for his second vice president. In 1940, the party's suzerains chose a Wall Street lawyer named Wendell Willkie to challenge Franklin Roosevelt. He had long been a Democrat, and had only changed his registration the year before. Much the same thing occurred in 1952, when GOP notables recruited Dwight Eisenhower, a recently retired five-star general. As a member of the military, he had never aligned with a party. So his turning into a Republican came even later than Donald Trump's switch.

Another difference, of course, was that Willkie and Eisenhower didn't spend upward of a year pursuing the nomination. As hardly needs saying, Donald Trump played rougher and tougher to get it than any contender in the history of the office.

It's often observed that late converts are more zealous than longtime sectarians. Whether or not this describes Trump, he has guided his office as a committed Republican. A measure of his fealty, as described earlier, was his forty-six rallies to get his partisans out for the 2018 midterms.

For all his braggadocio, just about everything associated with the Trump administration has been straight from the Republican textbook.

- His Department of Commerce sought to ensure that the census would contain a question on citizenship. Its aim was to deter recent residents from filling out the forms, which would inflate Republican representation at the state and federal levels.
- His Department of Education was giving for-profit colleges free rein to mislead their students and deny petitions for relief from loans.
- His officials in the Veterans Administration were earmarking more of the agency's funds for private providers.
- His Environmental Protection Administration allowed agribusiness to use pesticides, even those that inflict debilitating illnesses on their workers.
- His Department of Interior gave priority to opening national parks and federal lands to oil and gas extraction.
- His Department of Labor enabled businesses to define employees as contract workers, making them ineligible for benefits and predictable schedules.
- His Department of Health and Human Services created new barriers to limit access to abortion services.
- His Department of Defense obligingly redirected part of its budget for building a wall on the nation's Southern border. Nor did it object when he overturned criminal convictions by its tribunals.
- His Department of Justice recruited some 170 reliably Republican jurists, the better to reshape the courts over a generation to come.

- His Department of Agriculture told Republican states that their schools no longer have to put fresh fruits and vegetables on their cafeteria menus.
- His Federal Trade Commission's Republican majority fined Facebook a fleabite $5 billion for its egregious misconduct, without demanding that it overhaul its ways. (The firm's 2018 revenues were $55 million, while its market valuation has exceeded $500 billion.)
- Soon after yet another mass shooting, the president dimly ruminated about monitoring guns. Following a conclave with the National Rifle Association, nothing more was said or done on the subject.
- Republican stalwarts like the Chamber of Commerce and the American Enterprise Institute were conspicuously silent when the president installed tariffs, a posture the party had eschewed for almost three-quarters of a century.

Even early in his transition, it was manifest that Donald Trump would have no difficulty finding Republicans to staff his administration. Indeed, it's hard to name any who rejected such overtures or said they wouldn't serve. One wing of the party, its rank-and-file stalwarts, filled adoring arenas to urge him on, in turn giving the impression of a hefty "base." On another flank, all the Republicans in the Congress—the 293 who took office with him, the 252 who remained two years later—have given him just about everything he wants. It's not easy to find any who caviled over his priorities; the handful who did had already filed for retirement. Nor has there been public commentary from Wall Street magnates or Fortune 500 executives.

True, a half-hearted health bill failed to pass, due to three dissents in the Senate. In fact, its draft didn't originate in his White House, which only belatedly embraced it. More germane was the so-called Tax Cuts and Jobs Act, which was hastily enacted in December 2017. Who actually drafted that 1,097-page statute is still not fully known, nor does there appear to be any inclination to find out. More than anything, it was a wish list that businesses and the wealthy had been coveting for years. Few Republican administrations can boast of a statute that so wadded the wallets of the rich. It has skewed a maldistribution of income for the century away.

Not all Republican presidents are in the same mold. Even the two named George Bush differed in significant particulars. For example: caution versus bravado in Iraq. On this score, there's Donald Trump's obsession with tariffs. But that shouldn't have been a surprise. He had long vented his rage over other nations' fleecing a feckless United States. Plus his aversion to anything multi-national, expressed in rejecting the Iran and Paris accords. Indeed, it's worth recalling that an America First posture was an epochal Republican stance. So were draconian measures against migrants. Only an ocean-to-ocean wall is new.

To sustain a populist facade, Trump periodically snipes at specific firms. General Motors, AT&T, Harley-Davidson, and Merck have been targets. But none of the assaults have been followed by a press of presidential power. (A visible exception: his *Washington Post*–based vendetta against Jeff Bezos and Amazon.) Still, even if only verbal, this chastising is a change. Other than Theodore Roosevelt, over a century ago, it's hard to think of other Republican candidates or presidents who have publicly gone after prominent companies.

Another shift has been the banishing of the sobriquets *conservative* and *conservatism* after 2016. Since Barry Goldwater, that designation had been the official mantle of the party. At one point, Mitt Romney was advised to reassure his supporters that he was "severely conservative." In pursuing the 2016 nomination, Ted Cruz brandished his ideological card, hoping for resonance with regular Republicans. When the subject was raised with Donald Trump, he replied that he didn't like "labels," demoting a venerable ideology to a wardrobe tag. Aware of the narcissism of their new leader, Republicans shelved an idiom of long provenance.

Like every bid for reelection, 2020 will be a plebiscite on a sitting president. This year's ballots will also be a referendum on the nation's second-largest party. If ejecting Donald Trump from the Oval Office is foremost in most voters' minds, a close second is that they don't want Republicans governing them.

PART II
REPUBLICANS AND THEIR PARTY

As this book was getting underway, early in 2018, I contacted several websites where Republicans gather. I posted a simple request. I said I was writing a book that would in large measure be about them. Would they, I asked each one, tell me—at whatever length they liked—why they had chosen to be a Republican? (I also asked for the state where they lived.) Within a week, I had received over a thousand replies, long and short. Representative excerpts are at the bottom of the pages that follow. I'd like to thank them all for their time and effort, ideas and insights, candor and passion.

PART II
REPUBLICANS AND THEIR PARTY

18
THE CONCORDAT

Since the close of the Civil War, the GOP has been the party of wealth and profits. Its principal mission is to safeguard corporate assets, inherited fortunes, and investments of owners and executives.

This presents Republicans with a problem. The United States is ostensibly a democracy, which means majority sentiment must be given some heed. But the party's prime beneficiaries are a small sliver of the electorate, not enough to carry a few precincts. So to succeed at the polls, it has had to find other sources of support.

In considered steps, the GOP has expanded its portfolio, while not forsaking its solicitude for the well-to-do. Thus it has added policing of pregnancies and safeguarding firearms, embracing sectarian causes and purblind patriotism, along with undermining civil rights and unleashing local police. Republican candidates, from the presidency to county boards, not to mention judicial nominees, are expected to pronounce their support for these and kindred issues. If some seem like opportune conversions, all that is asked is an appearance of conviction.

Hence a concordat. On one side, its wealthy wing agrees to sit silently as women's clinics are closed and private arsenals are shielded. Urbane executives and financiers look in other directions when they hear xenophobic innuendoes and scientists being scorned. It is collateral for their upcoming bonuses and options.

The Republicans most align with my Christian values. (Nebraska)

In return, the party's less-affluent adherents concur with policies that enrich the party's affluent echelons, albeit at a material cost to themselves.[1] Under the concordat, both tiers get what they want most, at least when their party has power. This said, the GOP is finding that growing sectors of the country are repelled by both codicils to this agreement.

I agree with the basic values of the Republican Party.
I uphold Christian values and am pro-life. (Maryland)

19
A MEN'S DEN

As needs no saying, the major parties differ in discernible ways. While all generalizations are hazardous, some warrant a second hearing. Democrats are both more urban and urbane, an interplay of geography and personality. Republicans are typically older, more apt to be married, and ostensibly patriotic. While most Democrats are of European origin, each year sees them a smaller segment of the party, which is more prone to welcome colleagues of many races.

What's left is the basic gender division, even if it has a range of gradations, from physical to temperamental. The Republican Party is more a men's party. This overview holds, whether gauged by who occupies its leading positions or its sources of electoral support. The corollary is that the Democrats are more a women's party, also by the measures just mentioned.

Let's begin by positing that many women regard the GOP as their party and count themselves as its loyal supporters. According to CNN's 2018 tally, fully 23,419,789 gave their ballots to its candidates. On its own, that's not a negligible number.

The party has long had a roster of luminous women. At its head is Sarah Palin, who shared top billing on its 2008 ticket. A sample would include Michele Bachmann and Nikki Haley, Condoleezza Rice and Elizabeth Dole. Plus Ann Coulter, Laura Ingraham, and Kellyanne Conway. In earlier days, Oveta Culp Hobby, Margaret Chase Smith, and Phyllis Schlafly. Along with Sandra Day O'Connor, the first of her gender to serve on the Supreme Court.

America needs to have a strong military presence in other parts of the world.
(Nebraska)

Even so, this chapter's title will remain in place. It will propose that men not only dominate the party, but put their sexual stamp on its posture and policies. Its final analysis will be that the GOP is essentially an enterprise owned and overseen by men.

It can be easily demonstrated that men are more evident in GOP circles, especially when compared with Democrats. This holds among both rank-and-file voters and those in leading positions. Two examples:

- Since Sandra Day O'Connor's appointment, Republicans have filled nine Supreme Court seats. All went to men. Democrats had four vacancies. Of these, three went to women.
- For whatever reason, the Republican National Committee has not reported how many of its 2016 convention delegates were women. When the Democrats assembled, 61 percent were women.
- The table below shows the party divide on women's shares of 584 national and state offices at the start of 2019. In theory, the two parties could have had identical sexual quotients. (Indeed, both mandate that for seats on their national committees.) So it's appropriate to wonder *why* the ratios for Republican women span from less than half to below a third against those for Democrats. It's not that the parties impose quotas or ceilings. Rather, the incongruities arise from a less tangible ambience.

584 CAPITOL SEATS: JANUARY 2019				
Women's Share	*Senate*	*House*	*Governors*	*All*
Republicans	15%	12%	10%	13%
Democrats	36%	38%	29%	37%

If a sexual scale were wanted for the parties, we could do worse than use the final figures on the table. Republicans would rate a thirteen versus the Democrats' thirty-seven, as their shares of three sets of seats. An inevitable question has to be: why are Republican women so far behind? In the 2019 House of Representatives, the ratio was more graphic. Of the 102 women in that chamber, 89 were Democrats, leaving a baker's dozen Republicans. In

As a Christian, I can't in good conscience identify as a Democrat. (Alabama)

politics as elsewhere, prevailing ratios affect career choices. On the GOP side, women who enter its intramural forays—say, a primary for a legislative seat— are still likely to be cast as pioneers.

That's a view of the top. Equally important is the electorate itself: the tens of millions of citizens who, through varied activities, decide the postures of the parties and who will occupy public offices. Here the best template will be the 2018 midterm elections. At the top of state tickets, seventy-one governorships and Senate seats were at stake. Beneath them were the 435 seats for the House of Representatives, for which Democrats fielded 432 candidates, while the GOP settled for 397.

The table below gives gender breakdowns for the parties' total votes in House of Representatives races. The numbers come from synthesizing two sources. The first was the Clerk of the House of Representatives, who adds up all the parties' votes cast in 2018 contests. Those totals are in the middle of the table. (Minor parties received another 1,947,488 votes.)

The second source was the exit survey sponsored by CNN, in which citizens leaving the polls were asked if they would provide information about themselves. The first and most obvious item was their gender. The CNN survey had a large

VOTING BY SEX: 2018 MIDTERMS		
	Republicans	*Democrats*
Men	27,564,106	25,730,172
Women	23,419,789	34,997,426
	50,983,895	60,727,598
TWO WAYS TO SCAN THE ELECTORATE		
By Gender		**By Party**
Men		*Republicans*
Republican 51%		Men 54%
Democratic 47%		Women 46%
Women		*Democrats*
Republican 40%		Men 42%
Democratic 59%		Women 58%

I believe that Republicans are more logical, and tend to be kinder and more caring.
(West Virginia)

sample, and it is generally accepted as the best replica we have of everyone who voted. Its findings for men and women were applied to the actual electorate.

We can start by synthesizing these six numbers and hazarding some possible conclusions. Here are a few:

- If we analyze only the men, it turns out that 1,833,934 more of them voted for Republicans than favored Democrats. This is not a large gap. But when we look at the women, 11,577,637 more of them chose Democratic candidates. That's a partisan divide six times wider than for the men.

- Parsed another way, the Republican pool has 4,120,331 more men than women. While this is a noticeable number, it's not really large enough to stamp the GOP as a "men's" party. But on the Democratic side, women have a heavy majority, providing 58 percent of its votes. Arithmetically, they outnumber Democratic men by 9,154,578. It may be too soon to call the Democrats a "women's" party. As of 2019, they still held only 37 percent of its prime seats.

- The last last time most men voted Democratic was in 1964, when Lyndon Johnson smothered Barry Goldwater. Since then, they have been there for every Republican, from Richard Nixon to Donald Trump. The last time most women rallied around a Republican was in 1988, when 51 percent of them backed George H. W. Bush. After that, their most recent high was 48 percent in 2004, in reelecting the second Bush. Given these statistical declines, there is scant chance that women will ever again vote Republican in the same ratio as men.

CNN polls also asked voters about their household arrangements. Here, too, responses were revealing. Compared with Democrats, Republican women are more likely to be married. Overall, this would make them at least somewhat older and settled into a domestic pattern. (Of course, exceptions abound.) In 2018, Republican wives who had resident husbands outstripped single women by a margin of 80 percent. (For Democratic women, the married-single ratio was fifty-fifty.)

Liberals say you're too stupid to make a decision, unless you're in the elite. (Texas)

In this century, we are expected to presume that spouses have independent minds. So if or when a pair vote the same way, these will be independent choices or express an interactive influence. That noted, recasting CNN's findings shows a degree of connubial disagreement. Among Republican husbands as a group, fully 17 percent had wives who voted Democratic in 2018. By way of contrast, only 8 percent of Democratic wives had Republican husbands. Put another way, Democratic men seem to have more in common with their wives than Republican husbands do with theirs.

The most pronounced GOP paucity is single women. Less than a third of them voted Republican. This group subsumes all who haven't married, either lastingly or thus far, with those who are widowed or divorced. In the 2018 midterms, single women comprised 18 percent of the overall electorate; in marital terms, it's the fastest-growing group. Nor is it surprising that so many single women eschew the GOP. One cause, certainly, is their preference for the right to choose abortion, which only the Democrats are sponsoring. A related reason is their commitment to serious careers. If Republicans don't openly oppose such aspirations, it's not an option they champion. One more datum: among single Democrats, for every one hundred women, there are only sixty-four men. This doesn't bode well for intraparty pairing, dating, and mating.

Many commentators opined that Donald Trump, by his campaign and conduct, would alienate women. This may have seemed self-evident, given the bellicosity of his pronouncements, not to mention his gloating boasts of assaults.

But that wasn't the case on Election Day in 2016. In that year, 29,797,365 women voted for him, not a small number. More salient, this was only 1,424,567 short of their turnout for Mitt Romney four years earlier. This must mean that for every 1,000 women who supported a staid and stolid Mormon, fully 954 also filed a ballot for a raucous Trump. And they did so well aware of his attitudes toward their gender.

The Pew Research Center is quite possibly our most imaginative polling operation. Because they put a lot of thought into their questions, we hear more than opinions on personalities and issues. The Pew researchers offer us insights into elusive emotions that are rarely voiced aloud. (This is all the more

I'm a Republican because I believe other countries should respect our sovereign borders. (Kansas)

arresting, since the founding Pew family felt that such inquiries were a left-wing plot.)

Below is a question that the Pew Center asked a sample of Americans towards the end of 2018. A first reaction might be: why would anyone bother to open a subject like this? It's not as if *manliness* is a campaign issue or on legislative agendas. So I'll only report my own reaction. I found it helpful in expanding our understanding of the political parties. Here (slightly abridged) was the Pew question, and replies collated by sex and party affiliation.

Is it good or bad when people look up to men who are manly or masculine?[1]		
Saying "Good"	*Republicans*	*Democrats*
Men	85%	56%
Women	73%	45%
Saying "Bad"	*Republicans*	*Democrats*
Men	15%	42%
Women	24%	53%

As in all large-scale surveys, the question was simply presented to the respondents, with no elaborations or explanations. It's quite likely those answering had differing definitions, since *manly* and *masculine* can be construed in many ways. So it was left to each person to apply his or her own understanding of the key words, like whether to focus on physical aspects or less tangible expressions. A range might run from sexual stamina to battlefield valor, from airing perilous opinions to being loyal to a spouse. And it's possible that Republicans and Democrats ascribe different meanings to the words.

The most graphic finding is that so many Republicans of both sexes think highly of men they deem manly or masculine. That almost three-quarters of Republican women want their men to have that fiber isn't far below the number of men who hold that view about themselves. One inference might be that Republican women believe manly men should take charge and hence consent to male dominance in their party.

I love God and support school vouchers because most of the public schools are failing.
(Indiana)

Once this topic is on the table, several issues arise. For example, if some men rate high on manliness, we might conclude that others have a lower standing. Even that premise pokes a hornet's nest. It's wisest to pause before describing men who are putatively less manly as *feminine*. Considering some kind of continuum makes sense; even better, a multidimensional matrix. But this is a topic for another book.

With Democratic men, we are seeing something new and illuminating. Only 56 percent accept a depiction that for eons has been applied to their gender. Today, more than a few are willing to avow they are *feminists*.

As was seen among the 2018 votes cast for Democratic slates, 58 percent came from women and 42 percent from men. So these men seem willing to remain with a party where they are in the minority. And not just in statistical charts. In meetings, rallies, and other assemblages, they see themselves outnumbered, if not outranked, by the other sex. In 2018, Democrats ran 183 women for the House of Representatives, up from 120 just two years earlier.

Fewer Republican men are seeing seats going to the other sex. Of the women in major offices who were depicted earlier, Republicans held 35 seats to Democrats' 112. In the competition for candidacies, it could be that many Republican women are forbearing voluntarily, rather than being pushed aside. Recall their level of concern for sustaining the masculinity of men.

By way of contrast, less than half of Democratic women cast manliness in a good light. Here it would be illuminating to learn what induced this response. Anger over assaults and harassment are much in the air. Indeed, personal histories may be tingeing perceptions of politics. This and more noted, insofar as Democratic women want men to figure in their lives, apparently they look for other qualities in them.

In the past, building a business or a having an ascending career sufficed as a manly credential. Enough middle-class men could claim such success, even if it was attained inside offices, rather than working out in all weathers. One archetype was Herbert Hoover, an engineer turned millionaire. Or Dwight Eisenhower, an administrative general rather than a battlefield warrior. Mitt Romney, who made a fortune by buying and selling other people's companies, was judged man enough. That changed with the party's next candidate, who cleared the field, not least by disparaging the masculinity of his rivals.

Guns aren't the issue in horrible shootings, but the mental health of the individuals who use them. (New York)

At a rally a month before the 2016 vote, Trump made a brief but telling pitch for the masculine vote. As is widely known, much concern has been voiced about cranial injuries incurred by football players. Steps have been taken to ban especially damaging plays, require more protective helmets, and keep disabled players from returning to the field. For those who know and care, the key condition in question is called chronic traumatic encephalopathy.

In truth, we know the kind of spectacle lots of fans want. It is a rough-and-tumble, tearing ligaments, cracking bones, plus perpetual pain, not to mention ravaged brains. Athletes enter the arenas knowing the risks, which is one reason why they get outsized salaries, at least for their playing years.

Trump began by reminding his fellow fans of the sport's less regulated days. "You used to see those tackles, and it was incredible to watch." But, he continued, not so today: "Uh oh, got a little ding on the head? No, no, you can't play for the rest of the season! Football's become soft, like our country's become soft."

Here he was appealing to a demographic that sociologists have been slow to identify. More precisely, it is fans who voice their virility by cheering the smashing of skulls. If he could bring even a fraction of them to the polls, they would far outvote citizens who worry about, let alone can spell, chronic traumatic encephalopathy.

Policing, Prisons, and Pain. The Republican formula for deterring crime is punishment. In particular, it favors modes of incarceration so physically and mentally painful that inmates who are released won't want to risk being jailed again. Rehabilitation is seen as feminine, as are community policing and niceties about rights. States with heavy Republican voting correlate quite strongly with high incarceration rates. (For the statistically inclined, it's +0.523.) Hence, too, there is Republican disdain for Black Lives Matter sentiment, as such solicitude can force police to keep their firearms stowed away. Were a poll to be taken, it would be intriguing to see how many Republicans prefer that Blue Lives Matter take precedence.

Insouciance about Health. Republicans only grudgingly acquiesced to seat belt laws, another incursion of the "nanny state." Playing it safe is feminine; if

---

Excessive taxation for corporations pushes jobs overseas. (Virginia)

women want to buckle up, fine. But real men don't want to be tied down. Republicans object to forcing fruits and vegetables on school menus. A way to tutor middle-schoolers about liberty is to cast pizzas and sugary soda as rights. Counting calories is feminine. Robust Republican voting correlates with high obesity rates (+0.702).[2]

Nature: To Be Used and Subdued. Our nation was wrested from wilderness, and that struggle hasn't ceased. Fossil fuels are our current frontier. Slicing mountains, fracturing farmland, and allowing chemical runoff are masculine modes of releasing energy. Solar panels and wind turbines are feminine. Roustabouts in oil fields or offshore rigs are Republican archetypes, not bespectacled scientists poring over models. Moreover, manly labor deserves diversions. Like snowmobiling through national parks or muscular vehicles on coastal dunes. Even non-rural Republicans opt for pickup trucks. Electric cars are feminine.

Carnal License. Republicans' preferred religions are deeply moral about sex. For young people, abstinence should be the sole instruction. Or when that warning isn't heeded, the next step is to make all pregnancies end in birth. Which leads to another correlation with high Republican voting. Those states also lead in teenaged births, the great majority of which are not accompanied by marriage (+0.698). How might this be masculine? It takes two to make a conception. (Apparently, abstaining isn't working.) The GOP flourishes where men parade their prowess, even if it leaves women with the consequences. Still, high teen births in Republican states show moral consistency: with the abortion option withheld, one outcome is more early motherhood.

Liberals will allow more radical Muslims into this country. See what is happening in France and the United Kingdom. (Pennsylvania)

20
POLICING PREGNANCIES

In one aspect of its politics, the United States stands apart from other democracies. It is the only nation where a large portion of its population gears their votes to how candidates stand on abortion. That issue no longer divides Ireland, and is quiescent in France, Italy, and Spain, even with their Roman Catholic legacies.

Here a caveat is needed. In the United States, it is primarily citizens who *oppose* abortion who frame it as their core concern. For many, it easily tops their list. Even so, they are not a numerical majority. As we have seen, more than half of Americans want the procedure to be available, and to have this choice within reasonable reach. But few of them voice that sentiment with the intensity that drives the other side. Indeed, for most who support choice, it is one of many topics on which they have opinions. Nor is this an anomaly. Owners of private arsenals tend to be sharply focused and evince more passion than those supporting controls.

This chapter will be saying quite a bit about abortion, and for a reason. Since 1976, Republicans have set abolishing abortion at the center of their platform. For more than four decades, it has provided the party with a solid core of support. More to the point, its allegiance can be counted on regardless of whatever other stances the party affirms.

If abortion is most explicitly a medical or surgical procedure, it has become a lot more than that. Indeed, it's hard to think of another clinical practice that raises so many ramifications. Of course, it is about pregnancies, and how they should eventuate. It's also about a sexual activity that can lead to conception,

---

I see no problem with businesses or individuals giving as much politically as they choose. It's called free speech. (Georgia)

87

but which can be pursued for many other purposes. To this extent, opinions about abortion echo how people feel about carnal commingling. How far abortion is accessible, if at all, can expand or constrict the lives of women, with secondary consequences for men. Arguments about abortion turn intense because this procedure has become a surrogate for forebodings not always acknowledged or understood. As a public issue, it also allows individuals to define themselves morally and present who they are to the world.

One talisman is the GOP's view that teenagers should be taught denial: to curb their urges by remaining chaste until marriage. Allied to this precept is the belief that sexual release should be confined to licensed and loving partners when they intend to reproduce. Altogether, a source of Republican anxiety is that sex is suffusing our society, and to an unconscionable degree. Public discipline must be imposed to rein in wanton drives.

On abortion itself, the parties are deeply at odds. The 2012 Republican platform stated its position succinctly: "We assert the sanctity of human life and affirm that the unborn child has a fundamental individual right to life which cannot be infringed." The party's ultimate goal is to have the procedure totally banned, settling for erecting obstacles until that time comes. The Democrats in 2016 were just as direct: "Every woman should have access to quality reproductive health-care services, including safe and legal abortion." Also in 2016, even before Donald Trump had secured the nomination, Republican platform officials were framing its most sweeping abortion statement yet. It ran over nine hundred words, with paragraphs specifying *waiting periods*, *parental consent*, and *clinic regulation*. Along with deploring *fetal harvesting*, *early induction delivery*, and *dismemberment*, as well as *stem cell research*.

Other Republican qualms are closer to the surface. Stated simply, they see sex as an original sin. Lust, which features prominently on the Seven Deadly list, inheres in our corporeal condition. Hence its urges must be repressed and suppressed if humans are to lead productive and enlightened lives.

The parties' positions generally reflect the sentiments of their supporters. How people feel about abortion is expressed in the results of two surveys, which took different approaches in the questions they posed. Indeed, some pondering is needed to fathom what's going on in people's minds. As can be seen, 72 percent of Republicans take the pro-life position; yet only 66 percent

The best way to avoid wars is to be prepared for them. (Georgia)

OPINIONS ON ABORTION: CHOICE, LIFE, AND LEGALITY[1]		
"Would You Consider Yourself to Be Pro-Choice or Pro-Life?"		
	Republicans	*Democrats*
Choice	28%	71%
Life	72%	29%
	Republicans	*Democrats*
Legal	34%	86%
Illegal	66%	14%
No opinions or undecideds are omitted.		

want to make abortion illegal. With Democrats, the choice view gets 71 percent, but rises to 86 percent when the legal option is given. Equally notable is that as many as a third of Republicans want abortions to remain legal in most circumstances, not just rape and incest. Nor should this be surprising. At least a third of its supporters have other priorities, like taxes and immigration, or firearms and racial worries. They go along with the platform, just as those who put abortion first accede to stands on other subjects. On the whole, Democrats feel more benignly toward sex. Most believe its impulses will surface, even amid the most stringent of controls. (So best include condoms in curricula.) Against the GOP's stress on sanctity and self-control, Democrats propound what might be called *responsible sex*: fusing lust with respect, exhilaration with precautions. But given the frequency of couplings, with even the most sedulous safeguards, mishaps will occur. Hence most Democrats believe that provisions for ending pregnancies should be broadly available. While the phrase *abortion on demand* is never used, it is what is being espoused.

So here is the battle line. One party says childbirth must sometimes yield to other choices. The other views pregnancies as beyond debate; once begun they must be brought to completion. Abolition has been a central Republican tenet since 1976, with the first platform subsequent to the Supreme Court's 1973 decision in *Roe v. Wade*. All ensuing party pronouncements have called for barring the procedure, not just via legislation, but by embedding the ban in the national Constitution. In all parts of the country, nomination to Republican

---

Wide-open borders are what scare me most. (Virginia)

slates requires an avowal of opposition. Similar affirmations are expected with elected and appointed judgeships. It's not easy think of another topic—guns are close behind—where the GOP demands so adamant a stance.

On first reading, it might seem anomalous that a party whose prime priorities are wealth and profits would take on the policing of pregnancies. That it has says a lot about what Republicans will do to gain and maintain power.

At the outset, any analysis should grant that views about abortion can have religious wellsprings, especially if forms of worship interweave theology and ideology. When Americans take to religion, they are more apt to vent passions than in more settled societies.

As the 1970s started, concern over abortion was almost wholly a Roman Catholic province. As it happens, its tenet that gestation must take its course is not an ancient doctrine. In earlier times, the church countenanced terminations up to when the fetus became "animated," meaning that movement could be felt. In 1591, Pope Gregory XIV issued a papal bull positing that "unanimated" embryos lack a soul. This essentially said that they could be removed, as readily as a cyst from a liver. It was only in 1869, barely a century and a half before our time, that Pope Pius IX changed the rules, proclaiming that full life commences at conception. So the sanctity of a seconds-old embryo is a rather recent canon of an otherwise venerable church.

As recently as 1968, abortion wasn't on the agenda of most evangelical denominations. Bruce Waltke of the Dallas Theological Seminary affirmed a general consensus that year, when he wrote, "God does not regard the fetus as a soul, no matter how far gestation has progressed." For authority, he cited Exodus 21:22–24. This view was supported by the magazine *Christian Life*: "The Bible definitely pinpoints a difference in the value of a fetus and an adult."[2]

Yet changes were in the wind. Not long thereafter, in 1971, the Southern Baptist Convention affirmed "the sanctity [of] fetal life." Even so, its adherents included provisions for abortions "under such conditions as rape, incest, clear evidence of severe fetal deformity, and carefully ascertained evidence of the likelihood of damage to the emotional, mental, and physical health of the mother."[3]

The recession? Democrats gave mortgages to everyone who wanted them. (Georgia)

These allowances aren't far from Planned Parenthood's platform today. With the Baptists' codicils—especially the emotional and mental provisos—networks of clinics would still be needed.

A new era opened in 1973, when the Supreme Court gave federal approval to abortions in *Roe v. Wade*. That decision, a decree in the name of the national state, prompted a major shift in evangelical theology. A posture that had seemed somewhat relaxed, or at least ambiguous, became a rigid stance. Henceforward, the dictum would be that any germination creates a sacred soul. To purposefully end it should be considered murder.

The decision had another consequence. As recently as 1960, when John Kennedy ran for president, many Protestants were so deterred by his Roman Catholicism that they refused him their vote. Yet not much more than a dozen or so years later, an unusual détente was coming about. A critical mass of Protestants joined dutiful Catholics in a joint campaign to overturn *Roe*.

In 1972, Richard Nixon's platform did not speak of abortion at all. But not long thereafter, Watergate intervened and he subsequently resigned in disgrace. In 1976, a beleaguered GOP felt obliged to nominate Gerald Ford, his hapless successor. Republican prospects looked so dim that any straw was considered for grasping. One came from Jesse Helms, a North Carolina senator who was always avid for a decisive issue. He proposed that the party commit to revoking *Roe*.

So it's worth the space to parse the GOP's 1976 platform. The relevant section opened almost as an academic essay, notable for its even-handed tone:

> The question of abortion is one of the most difficult and controversial of our time. It is undoubtedly a moral and personal issue but it also involves complex questions relating to medical science and criminal justice. There are those in our Party who favor complete support for the Supreme Court decision which permits abortion on demand. There are others who share sincere convictions that the Supreme Court's decision must be changed by a constitutional amendment prohibiting all abortions. Others have yet to take a position, or they have assumed a stance somewhere in between polar positions. The Republican Party favors a continuance of the public dialogue . . .

Government gives out so much free stuff now, so there's no incentive to work.
(Georgia)

But its text did not stop there. Notice that the last sentence has no period at its end. As if new hands had commandeered the keyboard, there then came this concluding clause:

> . . . and supports the efforts of those who seek enactment of a constitutional amendment to restore protection of the right to life for unborn children.

So four decades ago, the GOP pledged to do all it could to end accessibility to abortions. Ronald Reagan's 1980 platform, after a nod to "differing views," sustained the 1976 affirmation, adding "we also support the Congressional efforts to restrict the use of taxpayers' dollars for abortion." A Republican Congress soon passed the so-called Hyde amendment, prohibiting federal funding for abortions. It has been subsequently renewed.

Fast-forward to 2016. Donald Trump, like many Republican aspirants, had earlier held the view that women had a right to choose. This had also been the case with Ronald Reagan, Mitt Romney, and the senior George Bush. But to obtain the nomination, all four proclaimed they had been converted to the anti- side. On this score, Trump went much further than any of his predecessors. In March 2016, he told MSNBC he felt that "some kind of punishment" should be inflicted on women who sought the procedure. Even right-to-life zealots were aghast. Their stance is that women who have had abortions are themselves victims of a barbaric system. Those who subsequently express regret are invited to join the opposition and are often featured in it. After going on record for overturning *Roe*, which would end federal involvement, Trump averred that women could "travel to another state." In a word, teenagers in Alabama could still fly up to Illinois.

As with other topics, Trump held forth with improvisations. So here he was in October, in his final debate with Hillary Clinton: "If you go with what Hillary is saying, in the ninth month, you can take the baby and rip the baby out of the womb of the mother just prior to the birth."

It's immaterial that neither Clinton nor anyone else has ever supported allowing interventions at so advanced a stage. Veracity was not how Donald Trump won his nomination or the margins that assured him the Oval Office.

Black Americans are told that capitalism is racism. (Virginia)

What's germane here is that "rip the baby" enthralled Republicans, who now had evidence that he was their man. His riffs on abortion galvanized rank-and-file Republicans more than anything John McCain, Mitt Romney, or either George Bush had essayed.

If a religious denomination includes conception in its theology, those joining its rolls are usually assumed to embrace that part of a creed. Still, religions are not totally doctrinal. They provide comfort, succor, and elucidation that goes beyond tenets and texts. Individuals have deep-seated needs that can be solaced by spiritual creeds. This chapter will consider some aspects of modern life that the abortion issue helps to resolve.

Republicans have always prided themselves on holding high standards for family life. By this it means marriage unto death, responsible raising of dutiful children, and eschewing unconventional sex. At least, this is its outward stance. In fact, prominent Republican seem as drawn to licentious couplings as any kindred group of Democrats. Three of its recent stalwarts—Newt Gingrich, Rudolph Giuliani, and Donald Trump—together boast nine betrothals and assorted infidelities. Also among the party's adulterers have been Dan Burton of Indiana, Mark Sanford of South Carolina, Bob Barr of Georgia, and Helen Chenoweth of Idaho, all from strong Republican states. Plus Henry Hyde of Illinois, John Ensign of Nevada, John Schmitz of California, and Tim Murphy of Pennsylvania, as well as both David Vitter and Robert Livingston from Louisiana.

So it may be that straying Republicans, whether in public or private spheres, have a special need to affirm their moral stature. An apt avenue is to espouse a strict conception of life. Virtually all humans want to believe that they are *moral* creatures. This desire goes well beyond sexual indiscretions. In today's United States, it isn't easy to satisfy ourselves that we are leading principled lives. If anything denotes this country, it is its stress on success and status, with plaudits for lauded talents and envied attainments. But with so much emphasis on the self, not much energy is left for commitment to the wider society. Of course, Americans can attest they've worked hard, paid taxes, and improved their neighborhoods. However, these are everyday expectations, warranting two cheers at best. But a third asks for evidence that you have denied yourself to aid others.

Low mobility among African Americans stems mainly from dependence on government. (Virginia)

Many, if not most, Republicans show little solicitude for people seen as short on initiative, responsibility, and effort. True, they support charities with suitable recipients. But all too many of those low on the social scale are seen as being culpable for their own plight. Hence Republican penchants for harsher prison sentences and limited assistance for the unemployed, not to mention heavy penalties for late loans. Given such agendas, those who take a stern line need an avenue for showing a caring countenance.

Enter solicitude for the unborn, as a way to establish that you are a moral individual. The right-to-life movement allows a broad band of citizens to feel that they are giving of themselves. Especially when they seek—as they often frame it—to rescue innocent infants from medical murder. Thus they can tell their grandchildren that they donated much of their vitality to fostering a more civilized and caring world. Few other causes offer so straightforward a satisfaction. If not all take time to picket clinics or resound at rallies, many send checks for causes such as underwriting counseling to those considering the procedure, to urge them from that choice. Each pregnancy that is preserved, by whatever means, is counted as an infant whose life has been saved.

An upside of opposing abortion is that the espousal itself will suffice. To that extent, it is a relatively undemanding way to gain moral stature. Thus adherents aren't expected to aid, let alone adopt, babies whose births they have induced. Nor are there signs that such opponents feel obliged to ponder the futures these children face. Republicans aren't notable for financing the schools these youngsters will attend, or the health care or other interventions that might give their lives a good start. It is as if the party's strictures on self-reliance commence at the moment of birth.

The centrality of abortion also excuses Republicans from another effort. By some moral logics, belief in the sanctity of life should lead to opposing executions performed in the public's name. But with so much involvement needed to oversee what happens in wombs, attention to capital punishment will have to wait. True, that all lives must be preserved (except in war) is still the official posture of the Roman Catholic Church. Yet it and other denominations that seek to end abortions do not show equal interest challenging to the death penalty. Few Republican officials have problems with capital sentencing, since it comes with the tough-on-crime menu. Research by James Unnever at the

---

Lower taxes, less bureaucracy, stronger national security, vigilance against terrorism, greater enforcement of criminal law, and competition in health care. (California)

University of Southern Florida found that of individuals who want to abolish abortions, over half also wish to preserve public executions.[4]

Nor do they see this as being inconsistent. But then, not many of us are ready to allow that views we hold may be logically dissonant. Hence humans become adept at weaving webs of words to reconcile positions we concomitantly endorse. Like: "The unborn are wholly blameless; murderers willfully transgress." At all events, it's far easier to champion a not-yet-born infant than adults slated for a gurney.

Since the dawn of human history, men have been aware of how women can challenge their domains. Even the haughtiest of men can be sensible to women's abilities and intellects. Yet not all men are comfortable amid talented women, especially if they become competitors. Hence the installation of impediments at every level. Most primitively, it was continual pregnancies and full-time household chores. Of course, this confinement is rarely espoused today. Even so, there remains an awareness of how pregnancies and their aftermath can limit women's lives. Of course, women now have more choice over if or when to have children. Hence an updating of older constraints.

Something similar is happening in higher education, where men now receive only forty-three of every one hundred bachelor's degrees, and even fewer at the graduate level. Insofar as those credentials are expected for advanced occupations, women may outpace men in appointments and promotions. Or look at a single school. When Yale admitted only men, it enrolled some 4,800 undergraduates, meaning that this number of men could embark with a Yale degree. Today, with coeducation and a slightly higher enrollment, it admits only 2,800 men and about the same number of women. As a result, out there now are 2,000 young men who once might have been Yale graduates and must now settle for less exalted degrees. To be sure, holding a Lehigh diploma is not the end of the world. But it's a descent from Yale. These downward trends for men can be multiplied nationwide. Might men want to revert to recurring pregnancies to remove women as competitors?

Igniting the issue allows the GOP to pit two pools of women against each other. On one side are those who tend to be younger and single, or older and divorced, and who seek to enjoy themselves sexually. This was a signal outcome of the 1960s sexual revolution, facilitated by the advent of effective birth

---

Private companies do a better job than government agencies can. (Texas)

control. Yet as noted, the more frequent the liaisons, the greater the chance of mishaps and unanticipated pregnancies. Here a corollary of sexual freedom for women is that abortions be broadly available. Indeed, only with its access can they have self-determination equal to that accorded to men.

Across from them are women, most of them married, who by choice or circumstance lead less venturesome lives. In their view, too much of what is occurring sexually is morally disquieting.

To them, easy access to abortion spurs hedonistic stirrings and imprudent couplings. For adhering to stricter precepts in their own lives, they have paid demanding dues. Yet out there, they see all too many of their gender cavorting with small risk of opprobrium or shame.

Much effort is devoted to parsing voters via conventional demographic categories, like income, education, or ethnicity. But could it be that Republican analysts have taken a more sophisticated turn, looking for indicators that are less susceptible to statistics? Of course, for many, abortion is a moral issue. But it can also rouse people beset by insecurities, anxieties, and anger.

I'm a decent human being and I believe strongly in the Second Amendment. (North Carolina)

21
IMPOSING NORMALITY

Most men and women describe themselves as heterosexual. That may well be an accurate assessment, at least in the present time. Nature has inscrutable ways of distributing traits and attributes. Hence there are more blonds than red-heads. And while nature countenances homosexual inclinations, thus far such individuals are a minor part of the population.

We have no realistic way of collating figures in this area. In May 2018, Gallup asked a large sample of adults, "Do you personally identify as lesbian, gay, bisexual, or transsexual?" Altogether, 4.5 percent replied affirmatively, with 3.9 percent of men and 5.1 percent of women. The poll did not break down the four variations. (An Australian survey had 3.4 percent reporting lesbian or gay, which might leave 1.1 percent for the other options.)[1]

An obvious question arises. How many people lied, as they often do with polls? It seems safe to surmise that more than a few men and women have had same-sex stirrings, fluctuating in frequency and intensity, even by chance and circumstance. Some may be much aware of these attractions, but prefer to keep them secret, not least to pollsters. In Psychology 101, we were taught to call this *suppression*, as with being aware of a condition, but outwardly denying it. Far more interesting is *repression*. Here we refuse to concede that something about ourselves even exists, whether from shame or fear or something more primordial. Indeed, much of the population may be unaware of being latently gay, lesbian, bisexual, queer, or uncertain about their gender. Needless to say, these realms are not amenable to percentages or statistics. Still, this chapter will look into what impels an insistence on unalloyed heterosexuality. Or on being wholly male or totally female.

I am pro-guns, anti-gay, anti-abortion, anti-tax, and anti-Muslim. (North Carolina)

The chief catalyst has been deciding who may marry. (An earlier focus was serving in the military.) The Republican position, as in its 2016 platform, heralds "traditional marriage and family, based on marriage between one man and one woman, is the foundation for a free society and has for millennia been entrusted with rearing children and instilling cultural values." The premise is that any man or woman may marry, so long as their partner is of another sex. So Republicans do not oppose homosexuals marrying. They don't disapprove if, say, a gay man weds a straight woman, as not infrequently happens. What they resist is giving the recognition of marriage to pairings of lesbian women or gay men.

Underlying this position is the conviction that homosexuality is inherently unnatural. On the premise that this is so, individuals with that identity are seen as a stratum whose members cannot claim general rights and protections, as in not being allowed to be police officers or kindergarten teachers, or to adopt children or obtain a marriage license. In this view, homosexuality is an unfortunate mutation. If it continues to persist, it should at least be denied official legitimacy. Others say they are only concerned with actual conduct, or as English jurists once put it, "carnal acts against the order of nature." Indeed, much aversion to same-sex pairings arises from fantasies conjuring what such couples might do in bed. Implicit in the GOP platform is a wish that homosexuality not exist.

As might be expected, when Republicans are polled, more oppose same-sex marriage than favor it. Yet the vote is closer than some people might think. A 2018 Gallup survey found that of those with opinions, 53 percent were against it and 47 percent were agreeable. Not the least reason is that many Republican parents have made peace with accepting that one of their children is gay.[2]

There's less ambiguity on the Democratic side. In the same survey, fully 80 percent favored opening nuptials to all adults. The tone of the party's 2016 platform gave a forthright endorsement. "Democrats applaud last year's decision by the Supreme Court that recognized LGBT people—like every other American—have the right to marry the person they love." It continued: "Democrats will fight for comprehensive federal non-discrimination protections for all LGBT Americans and push back against state efforts to discriminate against LGBT individuals."

Obamacare was a big step toward a socialistic system. (Virginia)

In sharp contrast, an underlying Republican premise is that heterosexual identity and comportment are the only normal states for the human species. In this view, other inclinations and activities are contrary to divine or natural dictates.

So it isn't asked why a considerable portion of the population eschews the heterosexual template. (Granted, a platform isn't a seminar.) There is no shortage of explanations, ranging from childhood seduction to overbearing parents, not to mention accusations of exhibitionism. If genetics have a role, Republican advice is to keep those propensities under wraps.

The GOP is not explicitly antigay. For those who are religious, all human creatures have souls and are eligible for redemption. In fact, most Republicans find it imprudent to be overtly homophobic, let alone vent an incensed aversion.

Thus the focus on marriage, which bestows official legitimacy on the unions they countenance. If Louisiana is made to authorize the uniting of two women or two men, it becomes an affirmation that homosexuality ranks equally with heterosexuality. If a cousin is united in a lesbian wedding, how is this to be explained to a six-year-old niece? Not many Republicans want to be put in a position of having to say that such rites are equally acceptable, let alone normal or natural.

The half of the Republicans who oppose such unions wish that heterosexuality would be the only human condition. Their view no longer has the preponderance it once did. But their party is sticking with them, and in return get their votes.

Islam is not a religion. It's a violent, radical crusade. (Virginia)

22

THE REPUBLICAN SOUTH

As few Americans need reminding, the South was a Democratic domain for most of its political history. In 1950, to select a sample year, 103 of its 105 seats in the House of Representatives were held by Democrats. (The other two were in Tennessee.) Its eleven governors and twenty-two senators were also from that party. Today, the region is almost as reliably Republican. No other assemblage of states has made so momentous a shift. So it's worth taking the time to learn how and why this happened and to ask whether, even with so grand a partisan pivot, Southern politics have basically changed.

The South has traditionally been delineated as the former Confederacy: Alabama, Arkansas, Florida, Georgia, Louisiana, Mississippi, North Carolina, South Carolina, Tennessee, Texas, and Virginia. But segments of Florida and Virginia are experiencing cultural changes, due mainly to migrations from more urbane states. Similar shifts are occurring in Texas and North Carolina, albeit at a slower pace. Added to which, Hispanics are now the principal minority in Florida and Texas, altering the dimensions of race and ethnicity.

The South has been America's most problematic region from its very beginning. Its spirit and structure were indelibly set when nineteen shackled Africans were taken ashore in Virginia in 1619. Viewed as property that could be bought and sold and punished, they became the root of the region's economy. The legal enslavement of living beings continued for almost two and a half centuries, and was only ended by a gory war. Yet its imprint, more than any other factor, still explains the texture and temper of today's South.

Islam is a sneaky dogma that is not a religion of peace. (Texas)

The choice of chattel labor gave it a pharaonic structure, more primitive than the vassalage of feudalism. Relying on trammeled sweat and muscle, there was no need to nurture the ingenuity that ignites innovation, as in pursuing the promise of technology. Even after bondage was ended, the South did not join the industrial age. It had manufacturing, of course, but not enough to lift the weight of the past. Our time has seen once-backward countries enter the modern world. Think Taiwan and South Korea. But this nation's South never fully shed the lethargy endemic to enslavement. That, as much as anything, is why it continues to have the lowest living standards in the nation. Indeed, by many measures, lower than in Taiwan and South Korea.

The importation of human cargos brought about a need by those of European lineage to differentiate themselves distinctly from those of African origin. Even with epithets like "rednecks," "crackers," and "trash," it was accepted that those deemed white were full members of the race.[1] More explicitly, there was the avowal that no white person, no matter how degraded, could ever be consigned to bondage. To this day, anyone viewed as white can gaze upon anyone deemed black, and muse: "Only your people were enslaved; mine could never be." Thus the surmise, still much alive in the South, that descendants of chattels are from a lower evolutionary level. Germans coined the term *Untermensch*. An American word wasn't needed. That's not quite right. The N-word served the purpose.

In the South, more than elsewhere, those who are endowed as white hold it as their most salient trait. If an assurance of white superiority was needed during slavery, that affirmation serves similar purposes today. Being regarded as white becomes especially important when the rest of one's life lacks recognition and promise. Southern whites, on average and in distribution, are visibly behind members of their race in the rest of the nation. This is evident in official indices. Whites residing in the South lead in infant deaths and teenage births, in lower incomes and lower rates of college completion, with more incarcerations and broken marriages. Also high are firearms deaths they inflict on one another, whether by homicide or happenstance.

Coincidentally, despite all efforts to preserve distinctions and division, racial disparities are actually narrower in the South. In South Carolina and Alabama, rates for black and white teenage births are only ten and eleven points apart.

I go to a shooting range once a month. (Georgia)

Up in Pennsylvania and Ohio, the racial divides are almost twice that. With household income, the races in Arkansas are twenty-five points closer to each other than they are in Illinois. These and other convergences spur Southern whites to look for other ways to affirm their superiority. If they are kept dispossessed, their race will serve as their solace. Today, Republican rule in the South at best makes token efforts to reduce its residual lag relative to the rest of the country. Public education and public health, to cite two examples, seldom rank high on its agendas.

As the 1960s got underway, it became clear that Southern Democrats were primed to deserting their national party. Until that time, it had been conceded that its Southern wing could build on an all-white electorate, while the rest of the party was becoming increasingly diverse. Clearly, that concordat couldn't last. The fifties brought the *Brown* decision banning segregated schools, which was met by a revanche to undercut that ruling. Northern Democrats, for their part, were aghast at fire hoses, attack dogs, and back-road executions.

Two events, both in 1964, ended the old Democratic détente. The first occurred during the convention that would nominate Lyndon Johnson for a full term. A motion was introduced to seat a delegation from Mississippi whose members were mostly black. While it failed, its very submission led the former Confederacy to conclude that Democrats were no longer an accommodating home. That fall, five of its states gave majorities to Barry Goldwater on the GOP ticket. (Such a breach had a trial run in 1948. Then, a similar bloc rejected Harry Truman in favor of a segregationist senator who had assembled a States' Rights slate.)

The other 1964 development was in Washington, where Northern Democrats used their congressional numbers to enact a national civil rights statute. Its focus was opening the franchise and was plainly aimed at the South. If few schools ended up desegregating, extending the ballot came quickly, not least because federal lawyers made it happen. (Plus voting was less traumatic than youngsters sitting side by side.)

Now able to vote, black citizens in the Southern states soon started to register, and they did so as Democrats. Nor was this surprising. Throughout the bulk of the region, the party was the only available platform. Even in 1964, Alabama, Arkansas, South Carolina, Louisiana, Mississippi, and Georgia were

---

I do not believe in unions. They lead to economic destruction. (Connecticut)

sending only Democrats to the House of Representatives. As a near-monopoly, the party had been the principal route to public office, and the vehicle for voters who sought an effective voice.

What happened next shouldn't have been startling, either. What do whites so often do, when even one or two black families appear in their neighborhoods or black children start attending their schools? The short answer is that they move out. Before the eyes of white Southerners, what had been their party was literally becoming integrated. But if you're going to move, you have to move somewhere.

The GOP acted swiftly. The mid-1960s saw the emergence of its "Southern Strategy," which invited whites of the region to switch their partisan allegiance. Almost all of them soon did. In public, they cited their loyalty to states' rights and limited government. Privately, the GOP offered a haven for whites seeking to escape racial mingling in their politics. Today, the South is the Republicans' firmest base. Together, its states averaged nine points higher for Donald Trump than his national edge.

It's not widely realized that by census counts, today's South is comfortably and dominantly white. Even in Georgia and Mississippi, which have the largest black populations, whites lead by twenty points. In outer states like Florida and Tennessee, whites are three-quarters of the total. So any analysis of the South should stress that it is predominantly a white region. Of course, black citizens have the vote. But they are isolated in what is seen as primarily their own party, the Democrats, whose ballots have little overall effect.

And here arises another calculation. Political folk wisdom says that parties seek to increase their share of votes by bringing new people to the polls. In theory, recruiting new adherents helps to attain and maintain power. This tactic has not been embraced in the South. Republicans have concluded that any effort to court black voters will backfire. For every five black citizens they might lure to GOP ranks, ten whites would leave. Since whites have comfortable majorities in all eleven states, the GOP sees no need to diversify its racial ranks.

White legislators have used their majority power to draw districts that hold black representation to the barest minimum. A glance at seven states—Alabama, Arkansas, Louisiana, Mississippi, North Carolina, South Carolina, and Tennessee—shows how that has been done. In these seven states, black

---

If more women were responsible with birth control, the abortion issue would decrease significantly. I'm female and a proud Republican. (New York)

residents make up 24 percent of the population. Together, the seven have been allotted fifty seats in the House of Representatives. Yet maps were so contrived that in only six—12 percent—could a black candidate be elected. Of course, there's no rule that seats must be racially proportional, or that voters must have officials of their own race. Still, the numbers are plain: 24 percent of the population gets 12 percent of the seats.

Needless to say, Republicans have always welcomed a handful of black conservatives, like South Carolina's Tim Scott. And of course Clarence Thomas. It would be astounding if of 40 million black Americans, some didn't choose to turn to the right. In a similar vein, the GOP can find enough Cuban Americans to give it a suitable Hispanic catchment.

Of course, there are other states where white Republicans hold key offices and dominate the voting rolls. Kansas, Nebraska, Wyoming, and Utah come to mind. The difference is that in these states, the principal race doesn't use its power to repress another that it outnumbers. The white South is not inclined to admit that the Civil War is over. In more than a few ways, they are redressing its outcome.

Republicans are the heart of America: down-to-earth, basic people. (Alabama)

23
A WHITE HAVEN

This chapter will be about race, one of the most difficult subjects to address with objectivity or clarity. What we see—or choose to see—is almost invariably clouded by emotions and interests. After all, we're talking about ourselves. But let me revise what I just wrote. Race isn't just a "subject." Whether we're confronting a reality or figments in our minds, what we conceive as races have consequences rewarding or encumbering actual human lives.

That said, there are no official definitions for what constitutes a race, let alone how many there are, or the boundaries for each one. So here are some guidelines this chapter will observe.

- For present purposes, the United States has two dominant races, usually called black and white, encompassing persons of African and European origin. They comprise the nation's most distinct racial divide. Of course, no one is literally or wholly black or white, but respective colors and complexions are distinctive enough to allow the division to persist. (Native Americans and Native Hawaiians can also be identified in racial terms.)
- Two other aggregations are not racial. *Hispanic* refers to a language, countries of origin, and a varied culture. But in physical appearance, Americans subsumed as Hispanic can evince European, African, and native ancestries, in many cases intermixed. Such diversity is even more vivid with an omnibus groups called *Asians.* The term subsumes not only Chinese, Japanese, and Koreans, but also Pakistanis, Filipinos, Saudis, and Yemenis, indeed everyone with forebears from anywhere in that gigantic continent. (Israel is also in Asia.)

Personal responsibility is what we need. (Minnesota)

- The artifacts we call races are human creations, crafted for a variety of reasons. This means they can also be erased if we choose. In fact, this has occurred. For many years, in many locales, it was common to speak of a "yellow" race. It handily embraced individuals of Chinese, Japanese, and Korean lineage. ("Oriental" and "mongoloid" were variants.) Yet soon after the end of World War II, the term fell from general usage. Those once in it were merged with many others under the aforementioned Asian umbrella.

- The epithet "racist" has been applied to some Republicans, due to broad pronouncements or policies they direct at groups like Mexicans or Muslims,[1] such as associating them with violence, whether conventional crime or acts of terrorism. It remains to add that neither Mexicans nor Muslims are races, since both encompass a range of cultures and colors. Such indictments, based on national and theological aspects, seem part of our time and are unlikely to disappear soon. So we may see racism being extended to include them.

- Now it's time to return to one of the races cited earlier. More than any of the others, it provides most of the impetus for the racial anxieties and enmities we see and hear. I am alluding to Americans deemed to be white. Many of these individuals of European origin feel grimly vulnerable. On one side, they sense hostility from their fellow citizens of African origin (as with athletes who don't kneel for the anthem); on the other, from arrivals from Latin America, the Middle East, and places with other languages, unfamiliar faiths, and darker hues. It's best to open with the black-white bifurcation and extend the analysis when applicable.

The Republican Party was founded in 1854. Barely a decade and a half later, it avowed its interracial identity. Nor was this surprising for the home of Abraham Lincoln. In homage to his death, its leaders amended the Constitution to secure the vote for Americans who had recently been freed from bondage. In ensuing decades, the party sent twenty-one men of African origin to the US Congress, all from former Confederate states. (Two were senators representing Mississippi.) But this was a short interlude. By the time the century had ended,

---

My ideal would be to completely cut off immigration. (Pennsylvania)

the region's white populace had regained its earlier domination. Under the Democratic Party of that time, black citizens were basically barred from political life.

Black citizens in Northern states could vote, and continued to cast their ballots for the GOP. That allegiance persisted through the presidency of Herbert Hoover. Even so, loyalty netted them only a single congressman, Oscar Stanton De Priest, who was elected from Chicago in 1928. Franklin Roosevelt's presidency brought a massive change. Black Americans outside the South shifted all but wholly to the Democratic side. Since then, the GOP has rarely roused black support exceeding single digits.

So for eight decades and counting, the Republicans have for all practical purposes been a white party. In vivid contrast, each year sees the Democrats becoming a multiracial and multiethnic coalition. In 2012 and 2016, whites provided only a bare majority—55 percent—of the votes cast for Barack Obama and Hillary Clinton.

On the nation's racial makeup, it's probably best to begin with the official count. The census allows individuals to describe themselves racially, and it simply records the responses it receives.

This makes sense, since in almost all cases, people give the designation that others would apply to them. In a 2018 count, the most detailed at this writing, just 60 percent of the overall population cited "white" as their sole identity. (Parents did it on behalf of children.) In doing so, they were attesting that all of their forebears had arrived from one or another country in Europe. So today, persons are considered fully white if their ancestors came anywhere from Spitsbergen to Salonika, with complexions from pale to tawny, and varied physical builds.

But note that the 60 percent for whites counts only individuals who are fully of European stock. To accord with current demography, the census has devised an accompanying category. It is available for individuals who might want to have Hispanic (or Latino) recorded as all or part of who or what they are. In 2018, fully 18 percent of Americans checked this box.

This was an all-time high, and it makes them the second-largest sector. Those who do check Hispanic or Latino have their own reasons. They may be saying that Spanish is their family's ancestral language. Or that their people are

---

Putting the interests of white Americans first and keeping our heritage is my most important reason for being a Republican. (Ohio)

from one of the countries composing Latin America. Or that they identify with a culture prevalent in that region. All that noted, it must be added that Hispanics vary widely in race. Some, as in Argentina and Chile, seem almost wholly of European stock. Others, as in the Dominican Republic and Cuba, have pronounced African origins. Many in Central America show strong indigenous antecedents. Peru has long had Spanish-speaking communities of Japanese origin, one of whom was elected the nation's president.

So now it must be added that among the 18 percent who say they are Hispanic, about two-thirds also check the white box. (Others say they are black; but even more leave it blank, averring they feel no need of a racial designation.) On paper, describing yourself as Hispanic-plus-white is analogous to those once called Irish American or Italian American. However, in the public purview, they are usually seen principally as Hispanic, and secondarily as white. As was just noted, this stricture no longer holds for citizens having European pasts. For them, being white has primacy, with a nationality sometimes but not always appended. Cases in point would be Samuel Alito and Antonin Scalia on the Supreme Court. No one has called them "Italian" jurists, although no one ignores that Clarence Thomas is black. So far, though, Hispanic heritage remains a barrier to being fully white. Ted Cruz and Marco Rubio have had to settle for this provisional status. At the same time, it needn't preclude the presidency, any more than having some African ancestry has. Indeed, the notion of being not quite fully white has a long history.

The original Republicans were predominantly of English, Scottish, and Welsh extraction. In an earlier generation, Alexis de Tocqueville had denominated them "Anglo-Americans." In many ways, that phrase still bespeaks the party's prototype. Its first demographic challenge came with Germans, who had began arriving before the Civil War. At first, there was concern that absorbing them might undercut the Anglo paradigm. But Germans were predominantly Protestant. They soon learned English, and many intermarried or modified their names. A rite of passage was serving in the Union army, easing their entry into Republican ranks. Their presence, along with sundry Scandinavians, helped give the party successive majorities from 1864 through 1928.

There are too many things we need to take care of first before allowing immigrants to come into this country and receive all kinds of services. (California)

All the while, though, immigration was taking another turn. Another great wave came from Ireland, spurred by destitution and religious subordination. They created a dilemma for Republicans. Ireland was a Northern European province, with English as its official language, albeit carrying a distinctive accent. True, too, they weren't Protestants; but German Catholics were fitting in. The problem was racial, even if that term wasn't used. Republicans found it beyond their reckoning to think of the Irish as fully white. That mood was caught in two depictions by Thomas Nast on an 1876 magazine cover, pictured below. On one side was a liberated black man, with a beguiling face. Across from him was a scruffy man, with subhuman features, and clearly of Irish origins. In a sardonic gesture, Nast wrote "white" under the second figure, as if to convey he had even less claim to that marque than the black man across from him. In a word, the Irish weren't white enough for Republican recognition. They, along with Southern and Eastern Europeans and other strains, could be consigned to the Democrats.

But that hauteur couldn't hold. The arrival and integration of immigrants enlarged the electoral rolls. Most pointedly, there were no longer enough whites of Anglo aspect to assure majorities for the Republicans. Indeed, in that 1864–1928 span, Democrats had higher presidential pluralities on six occasions. Still, out of pride or principle, the Republican Party sought to keep its white identity. Social developments made this possible by providing an opening. The end of World War II saw a mushrooming of subsidized suburbs, with many of the newcomers arriving from older immigrant neighborhoods. To facilitate this process, those once disdained as lesser breeds—as the Irish had been—were given a transitional status, variously called "white ethnics" and " hyphenated Americans." In a word, the white party was recasting its racial parameters, most distinctly during the Nixon and Reagan presidencies. (Not coincidentally, both had parvenu origins.)

Americans of Irish and Italian stock found they were welcomed by the party, as were Poles and Greeks, Slovenians and Lithuanians. By the time the twentieth century had ended, allusions to ethnicity and hyphens were hardly heard. So by erasing intermediate gradations, the party could now address its constituents as a common bloc. A singular white race, melding all European origins, eclipsed national divisions.[2] It remains to be seen whether and how far

---

When the government helps the poor, it shields them from the consequences of the bad decisions that made them poor. (Indiana)

Credit: American Antiquarian Society's Historical Periodicals Collection

It's all about pro-life. This tops every other issue or agenda. (Florida)

Republicans will expand their white parameters. Until now, their most notable additions have been Cuban Americans of their exile generation. There have been no moves to give Asians some kind of white standing, nor are there signs they want it. It will be revealing to see what designations are bestowed on offspring with Asian and white parents.

Each year finds the white portion of the population declining. The most visible cause is the current flow of immigration. Today, few Europeans want to move permanently to the United States, because they like living where they are. Instead, Latin Americans and Asians lead the list, with the Middle East not far behind. Each annual census shows the United States to be less white. As noted, their latest count was 60 percent, well down from a high of 90 percent as recently as 1950.

A second cause of white decline is that its adults are not producing enough infants to sustain their numbers. A basic demographic dictum is that every one hundred women in a group must have at least two hundred children to replicate their share of the species. Natality figures released in 2018 reported that each 100 white women were having 164 children.[3] This means that many couples are stopping at one child, or having none at all, which together diminishes the white ratio. Not the least reason is that youngsters are more expensive than ever, given the many amenities they are expected to have. Another is that more men and women are deciding that parenthood isn't for them, or are finding it's too late to start.

A common Republican charge is that Democrats focus on "identity politics."[4-5] For example, its stress on attributes like gender, disability, and sexual orientation. Instead, it is argued, voters should be addressed as Americans and citizens, with a common stake in national prosperity and security. Hence too the party's embrace of patriotism, hands over hearts, and flags in lapels. Still, the issue of identity raises a question. Isn't affirming one's self as white also avowing an identity? At 60 percent of the population, whites aren't a minority, although their 52 percent of births—today's babies are tomorrow's population—shows they are only a few points from that status. Not to mention that they are now down to 30 percent of the student body at UCLA and 28 percent at Berkeley.

When you hold someone responsible for their immoral or criminal conduct, that usually means punishing them. The left is willing to soften punishment, based on extenuating circumstances. (Indiana)

Pastors often find they can base their sermons on one Biblical passage, say, Exodus 6:27 or Matthew 3:14. In the same vein, responses to a single survey question can expose apprehensions and anxieties that are rarely voiced, let alone debated and discussed. An example was posed by the Public Religion Research Institute, in the spring of 2017, to a sample of white adults. Here were its findings:

Today, discrimination against whites has become as big a problem as discrimination against blacks and other minorities.[6]	
White Republicans Agreeing	73%
White Democrats Agreeing	30%

An initial reaction might be puzzlement. Why, it may be wondered, do so many white Republicans see themselves as facing bias based on their race? Nor is this all. They see this prejudice as oppressive as that faced by conventional minorities. And it remains to ponder why so many fewer white Democrats feel so aggrieved.

By objective measures, Republicans are doing quite well, with the party's center of gravity well up in the middle class. Over a third of its 2018 voters had incomes over $100,000. Plus a hearty 80 percent had attended or completed college, a hallmark of at least modest success. These indices prompt a two-part question: who is victimizing white Republicans, and what forms does this bias take?

It is altogether true that under affirmative action, whites have been on the losing end, as when they may feel that a position they sought was given to another applicant in the name of diversity. When this occurs, it becomes more than a onetime episode; there's a multiplied effect.

Suppose that a police department is hiring a new chief. Imagine that twenty-four of the twenty-six applicants are white and two are black. Posit further that the search ends with hiring one of the black candidates. Due to that decision, all of the two dozen white entrants can come away suspecting that a race-based choice impeded their careers. In other words, all it takes is just one black appointment to lead twenty-four whites to feel they suffered discrimination. Even whites contending for traditionally well-paid

I believe we are responsible for our own success. (Texas)

posts—say, a college presidency—can imagine they faced barriers based on their race.

If most Republicans feel they are being treated unjustly—as the survey attests—there is little point in trying to persuade them that this isn't the case. It is striking that seven of ten white Republicans are equating their own situation with groups that have long been subjected to suppression. And they hold this view at a time when Americans of European stock still preponderate in the population, even more in the electorate, and especially in regions where the GOP prevails. So it remains to ask what prompts their distress and whom they believe might be benefiting in their stead.

In fact, whites who say they encounter discrimination could be employing this term to vent another complaint. For most of this nation's history, white citizens of all conditions were allowed, if not encouraged, to see themselves as embodying a superior human strain. Knowing they were construed as white sufficed for millions of men to face death for the Confederate cause.

So to be deemed white has been to possess an existential asset, an attribution that has solaced millions of ordinary lives. In fact, for many of modest status, this ascription has been their most crucial advantage. Moreover, it was an identity its owner could never lose. (Historically, in Europe and the Americas, no white person, no matter how debased, could ever be consigned to slavery.)

Republican responses to the survey bespeak a lament over losing pride of place in the national scheme. To be sure, European lineage still has considerable stature. Norwegian origins open more doors than Nicaraguan parentage. Even so, European lineage does not command a deference it was once accorded. So when white Republicans say they face prejudice, they are saying that their race no longer affords the esteem earlier generations enjoyed. Or the preferment they feel is their due.

A 73 percent response rate doesn't occur overnight. It's likely this racial festering has been growing for a considerable time. Even so, established candidates like John McCain, Mitt Romney, and the younger Bush forbore from fomenting race-based resentments. (However, the senior Bush famously did.)

It took the unexpected arrival of Donald Trump to bring white grievances closer to the surface. Thus race was one of several readings for his pledge to Make America Great Again. Of course, it promised a renewal of the nation's

---

Immigration needs to be cut. Jobs need to stay here. (North Carolina)

industrial and military might. But it was also read as restoring the stature that citizens of European stock once had. The "again" was heard as reproducing a past era, a pledge that white Americans would regain their preeminence. If Hillary Clinton was the nominal opponent in 2016, a coequal adversary was Barack Obama's eight years of residence in the White House. This animus rose less from his supposedly radical policies than from his African background. If a disquiet was never openly acknowledged, to be governed by a man of his heritage was deeply demeaning to scions of a superior civilization.

It's not just that many whites still regard persons of another race as being innately inferior. Their African ancestry is a reminder that the nation was built on enslavement, a discomfort that will not readily go away. At the least, Republicans call for a cessation of racial accusations, protests, and complaints. Witness the sharp reactions to the phrase Black Lives Matter and kneeling football players. If we must have descendants of enslaved persons in our midst, why can't there be recognition of progress, if not some murmurs of gratitude?

Almost as intense are alarms over newcomers, relatively few of whom can be counted as white or black. Much Republican derision is attuned to nationality and religion, as with Mexicans and Muslims, albeit for different reasons. With the former, the unease is economic and cultural, over an undercutting of wages and a disinclination to assimilate. With Muslims reactions to unusual creeds mingle with fears of terrorism. While a race can't be strictly applied to Salvadorans or Palestinians, the passions they rouse parallel those with racial roots.[7]

Why are so many fewer white Democrats worried about the declining standing of their race? As noted earlier, they and white Republicans have somewhat similar educational and economic profiles. (Although Democratic rolls have more minorities with lower incomes.) On the material side, of those earning $200,000 and up, 51 percent went for Trump, and 49 percent supported Clinton, close to a statistical tie. The partisan divide within the well-off says much about our times.

It may be that white Democrats are more personally secure, with less need for race to figure in their lives. Or they may not see their careers threatened by demographic shifts. We can say that white Democrats—from union members to wealthy celebrities—knowingly participate in a multiracial party. In fact, it

---

By adopting America First, the Republican Party represents all Americans without dividing everyone into identity groups. (Michigan)

is one where they barely hold sway. As has been noted, whites accounted for only 55 percent of Democratic voters in 2018, while in the GOP they made up 88 percent.

So white Democrats have consciously chosen a diverse party. At its 2016 convention, black delegates comprised fully one quarter of those present, double their number in the general population. By contrast, the GOP could only muster eighteen black delegates, less than 1 percent of the 2,472 who were present. That the party made no effort to increase that number, if only to present a more diverse face, bespeaks its contentment with its white core.

We need to stop the homosexuals from infecting the earth with their ungodly principles. (Rhode Island)

24

ANTI–AFFIRMATIVE ACTION

A perennial Republican plaint is that appointed judges often impose decisions which have the scope of laws. In so acting, they usurp the province of elected legislators. Among much cited cases are the *Roe* ruling on abortion and *Obergefell* on same-sex marriage. This chapter will focus on another area where Republicans feel aggrieved. This is affirmative action. As the party construes such programs, they give special attention to individuals based on race, ethnicity or attributes like physical disabilities.

Affirmative action has long been combated terrain. Yet the most troubling issues remain beneath the surface, because they abrade sensitivities on all sides. The pages that follow will show why Republicans feel so vehemently about these policies. The contention generally centers on how admissions are decided at selective colleges and universities. It can also highlight employment practices, although this is not as high on the GOP's agenda.

The most recent decision was handed down in June 2016, as *Fisher v. University of Texas*. By a 4–3 vote, it rebuffed yet another Republican effort to end preferential programs. The case was also significant for the fervor of the dissents, which expounded on how minority admissions affect white candidates.

Abigail Fisher had been rejected by the University of Texas. She argued that this only occurred because she was white. The same claim had been made in earlier cases by plaintiffs Marco DeFunis (1974), Allan Bakke (1978), Barbara Grutter (2003), and Jennifer Gratz (also 2003). All their suits ended with ambiguous findings, which tentatively upheld affirmative action and lengthened

---

Liberals are elitist. Republicans are better at protecting America. (Kansas)

its life. Fisher's attorneys contended that she had a better academic record than most of the black and Hispanic students whom Texas had admitted. The university conceded it had lowered some bars, but cited "the educational benefits of diversity" as a greater benefit.

Fisher's appeal was sponsored, as had been prior cases, by Republican lawyers, with generous funding from donors linked to the party. So it's germane to ask why these pleas gained so much attention. After all, the admissions practices of selective colleges do not head most ideological or policy agendas. Clearly, more is involved than whether some teenaged applicants didn't get their first choice.

Fisher's petition was supported by Justice Samuel Alito, along with John Roberts and Clarence Thomas.[1] Their position was that white persons also have civil rights, and Fisher's had been abridged due to her race. Alito opened by citing as precedent a venerable dictum that "distinctions between citizens solely because of their ancestry are by their very nature odious to a free people." He went on to argue that the use of "race-based admissions" by the university, by itself, created "systematic racial discrimination."[2] Fisher had been refused her earned place because of an ancestry, which in her case was white, over which she had no control. The decision of the admissions office to "favor" (Alito's term) blacks and Hispanic applicants was what took away her college seat.[3]

When Fisher applied in 2008, Texas chose to admit approximately seven thousand of its white applicants for the year's entering class. The sheer size of that white intake suggests that she did not rank high on their "white list." (Of course, Texas and other colleges use such compilations.) Defunis, Bakke, Grutter, and Gratz also rated low among white applicants where they applied.

This explains why the GOP is devoting so much time and energy to battling programs that favor other-than-white candidates. In doing so, it is staging itself as a champion for whites who lack stellar credentials. America is probably the most competitive nation on earth, where the vying never ceases. Needless to say, not everyone can make the winners' circle. But what is even more demeaning is to open rejection letters, when you know there was a time when individuals of your ancestry were less likely to receive them.

My religion tells me that Republicanism is the only correct political party. (Utah)

As the table below shows, a generation ago, in 1980, white students filled fully 87 percent of the undergraduate seats at the University of Texas. By 2016, the year the Supreme Court ruled, their share was down to 48 percent. By a year later, as the table also notes, they had sunk to 42 percent, less than half their 1980 ratio. (Of course, the general population has been changing. But not as much as the college configurations.)

Whites on the Austin campus are now a minority, outnumbered by the other ethnicities taken together. Indeed, it is highly likely that more than a few white parents who themselves had been readily accepted by Texas were seeing their offspring turned down.

Of course, these sensations of deprivation are not mentioned in the affirmative action debate, by Justice Alito or anyone on either side. The table below shows how far places once reserved for whites are being accorded to two other groups. One combines black and Hispanic applicants, who are the chief beneficiaries of affirmative action. The other group consists of Asians, who rarely get or need such preferences, if only because they tend to have strong academic records.

COLLEGES: CHANGING COMPOSITIONS				
	1980	2018		
	White	White	Black–Latin	Asian
Texas	87%	42%	27%	21%
Michigan	89%	60%	10%	14%
Amherst	88%	44%	24%	14%
Yale	83%	45%	20%	18%
Stanford	73%	36%	23%	22%
Chicago	80%	42%	18%	18%

A problem white applicants and their parents face is that they can't openly protest that more places are now being given to high-scoring competitors with names like Chan and Kim and Singh. In the past, it might be murmured that Asians fell short on athletics or fraternity affiliations, or that they spent more of their time studying. But such ripostes are unseemly in a meritocratic age.

I believe all LGBT people are sinners and do not deserve the same rights as any normal person. (Arkansas)

(Michigan's percentages differ because a 2006 referendum banned affirmative action in the state.)

So the one way left to regain places whites have lost is to target black and Hispanic students, who are often let in with less prepossessing credentials. And there's another factor in college admissions, which involves an issue that whites prefer to keep under wraps. It's telling that suits akin to Fisher's have not been filed against preferences given to whites who are not academic stars, such as those whose parents had attended the college, commonly called "legacies." Or others who are adept in sports like tennis, hockey, and golf, where proficiency is honed in well-endowed suburban and private schools. Nor is it surprising that Republicans haven't filed such cases. Such suits would bring a spectacle of whites suing whites.

A related and equally undiscussed issue is downward mobility. Given white rejections attendant to affirmation action, it is a hazard haunting even professional households. Fisher's suit catered to white Texans, a strong GOP cadre, who were seeing diminished prospects for their children. It's as if the data on our table is never far from their minds. Some other figures supplement the story.

One touches on Princeton applicants whose parents previously attended. Currently, only about one in three of these putative legacies is being accepted. So for a substantial pool of mothers and fathers who themselves had been deemed of Princeton quality, two-thirds of their progeny aren't getting that nod. Of course, not all children measure up to their parents. (It would be a genetic oddity if they did.) Nor will it be the end of the world for those who were turned down. They will doubtless end up at respectable schools like Hamilton or Macalester. By objective measures, such places are perfectly fine. Yet in the competitive maelstrom, their degrees carry less weight. The sociological bottom line is that these and children like them will enter adulthood a step below their Ivied parents.

A Brookings Institution study examined young people who were raised in households with incomes in the top 20 percent of all earners. (For a comparison, in 2018, such families had incomes of at least $126,855.)[4] We may presume that as children, they attended good schools and had other advantages money can buy. Researchers tracked these youngsters into their adult years to

---

I believe in a strong unified America with a strong military presence around the world.
(California)

see how they ended up. Given how parents invest in their children, it's apposite to inquire about the payoff. Of these offspring who began with a strong start, only 37 percent ended in the top fifth themselves. All the rest, a considerable majority, had moved down the social scale. Insofar as America purports to laud opportunity, mobility is a stern mistress. The top quintile can't take in more than a fifth. It decrees that for each person who moves up, another will have to stumble or tumble, including many who started with silver spoons.

Climate is always changing. It's being used as a Trojan horse for a global agenda.
(Georgia)

25
COLLEGES, CLIMATE, AND OTHER CHIMERAS

In 2017, the Pew Research Center solicited public views on higher education. This was the question they posed: "Would you say that colleges and universities have a positive or a negative effect on the way things are going in this country?"[1]

At first reading, this might seem a curious question. One wouldn't look for deep doubts regarding shopping malls or the real estate profession. But the Pew analysts seemed to sense there was an issue here. It turns out that they were on to something. Here is what they found. To start, well over half of Republicans—64 percent—felt that colleges and universities were having an adverse impact on the surrounding society. Only 21 percent of Democrats held that view. As in many surveys, those replying weren't asked for the reasons behind their views. Still, we may surmise that this many Republicans have misgivings, both about what colleges are teaching and research emanating from universities.

Many Republicans have attended college, but the Pew study didn't ask people to evaluate their own experiences. Rather, it solicited their view on the impact of higher learning on the country. So let's look at some activities associated with academe. One college boasts majors in restaurant management and fashion merchandising. Another offers a seminar on *Moby-Dick*. A third conducts research on pesticides, and a fourth fields a lauded football team. A fifth relies heavily on underpaid adjuncts, while many of its students pile up lifelong debts.

Some Republicans may feel that one or more of these undertakings actually harm the larger society. (Should $150,000/year professors be devoting a

Republican policies align closer to Biblical morals and values than any other party.
(Oklahoma)

semester to a whale?) But it's unlikely that many Republicans have the minutiae of campus life in mind. Rather, their animus toward higher education is part of a more general appraisal of the media, entertainment, and other clusters they see as liberal or left. If they know one thing about colleges, it is that most professors vote Democratic, and that the majority of campuses veer toward a progressive consensus.

So what riles Republicans is the tenor and content of what is being taught and learned. As most of them see it, what is being imparted is not even knowledge, but left-leaning ideology. (That excursion in *Moby-Dick* is a critique of late-colonial capitalism.) Even worse, a pretense of objectivity cloaks a vapid amorality. Republicans will affirm respect for the realm of the intellect, as and where they can find it. (Hillsdale College, for instance, or Liberty University.) But the colleges and universities they see aren't even promoting the interplay needed for open scholarship. Where are affirmative-action searches for Pentecostals and Southern Baptists?

Most universities are associated with advanced research. Yet there is reason to believe that Republicans are as mistrustful about what emerges from laboratories as, say, classes in ethnic studies. Indeed, a similar skepticism dismisses whole areas of scientific knowledge. (For those so inclined, there are websites citing alternative scientists to reinforce their misgivings.) Perhaps the most prominent examples are dismissals of findings from the science of climatology. Accredited scholars in this field are essentially unanimous in agreeing on two truths. One is that global warming and climate change are imperiling the entire planet. The second is that human beings, due to their inventions and activities, are the chief cause of this portentous condition. As was noted earlier, most Democrats accept the scientists' conclusions and warnings. Most Republicans do not.

How to explain such substantial Republican rejections of what scientists are saying? To address that question, one fact should be put on the table. It is that both parties have sizable catchments of college graduates. Having such a core could explain Democrats' opinions. After all, an aim of higher education is to instill respect for research on the natural world. So we're left with explaining why many Republicans with similar schooling remain so suspicious. For one thing, there's the notion that the sentiments of citizens can and should carry

---

Our right to own guns shouldn't be stripped because of a few psychos who don't know how to control themselves. (New York)

equal weight with those of supposed experts. Insofar as Republicans take this view, they are espousing a form of democracy: that proverbial people in the street are as perceptive as those with acclaimed credentials. Apparently, Republicans regard climate scientists much as they do sociologists and literary critics. In a word, just another knot of academic ideologues. Hence a suspicion that data is being distorted and findings overstated to fit partisan postures.

Is there an alternative science? Somewhat over half—53 percent—of Republicans agree that "humans have always had their present form."[2] Presumably, this means that *Homo sapiens* appeared as a fully formed handiwork, not through stages in a long process. By contrast, 71 percent of Democrats accept that "human beings have evolved over time." Few in the GOP now demand that Darwin be stricken from curricula. Rather, the mantra is "teach the controversy." Its phrasing intimates that evolution is still an open theory, so divine creation and intelligent design deserve comparable classroom time. Course materials are available from organizations like the Institute for Creation Research. Similarly, those challenging warnings on climate change can obtain syllabi, replete with doctoral citations, from the Heartland Institute and the Competitive Enterprise Institute.

Across the political spectrum, people generally believe what they want to believe. Once they have chosen how they see the world and what makes it turn, they select supportive material to strengthen that stance. There are Republican reasons for their reactions. The charge that human excesses are wreaking baleful consequences threatens entrenched interests. The current chief executive has called such tocsins a "hoax," echoing sundry legislators. It also explains why no Republican demurrals were heard when their president withdrew the United States from the Paris Climate Agreement.

Two more surveys add some dimensions. One asked individuals: "In your view, is the seriousness of global warming generally exaggerated?" Here opinions are being solicited; even more, their beliefs about actual conditions. Among Republicans, 75 percent took an exaggeration position, disdaining what most scientists are saying. On the Democrat side, 15 percent checked that box. A second study simply asked people: "Do you worry a great deal about climate change?" Among Republicans, 82 percent said they did not, against the 34 percent of Democrats who shared that serenity.[3-4]

Those who fail have decided not to take advantage of opportunities. (Indiana)

The GOP has long been the party of fossil fuels. Hence its dominance in an arc extending from Kentucky and West Virginia, through Oklahoma and Texas, and up to Wyoming and North Dakota. Al Gore may fulminate that the prognosis for the planet is dire, but Republicans have decided not to lend such broadsides their ears. In its heartland, and much of elsewhere, business bottom lines feature profits garnered from oil and gas and coal. From early days, enterprises have sought free rein to exploit whatever natural resources will enhance their balance sheets. This explains the Republicans' lack of chagrin over polluted streams and fractured farmlands. The sight of smokestacks spewing fumes attests to an abundance of robust work. That sea levels may be rising by a few inches is dismissed as casuistic alarm.

Since climate itself is so ephemeral, confronting it is unlike other issues. Of course, environmental disquiet is not totally new. At one time, acid rain was on agendas, as was cleaning waterways. But the climatic indictment surpasses any in the past. Citizens are aware they will be asked to change more of the ways they live than ever before. In particular, they face being told to curb pleasures and amenities that are woven into their lives. This regimen would also expand the powers of official agencies, always anathema to Republicans. More rulings bring increased compliance costs, which undercut profits. Nor are businesses the only ones to cavil. Owners of guzzling vehicles and commodious homes would face rising assessments geared to carbon emissions.

Addressing climate and its consequences will be expensive. Bottled water, for example, could double in cost if all of those plastic cylinders are to be ecologically disposed. Not to mention new taxes for an array of public facilities. Here, it hardly needs saying, partisans differ. But in one respect they are similar. In 2018, individuals with incomes over $100,000 accounted for 47 percent of Democratic votes and 52 percent of Republican votes. So both are well-represented in a tier susceptible to higher taxes. Yet when surveyed that year, 72 percent of Republicans felt the taxes they had to pay were too high, whereas only 44 percent of Democrats made that complaint.

So let's posit two households, giving them both incomes of $150,000. At last reckoning, such families are expected to average $17,863 in federal income taxes. In one home, its residents are steadfast Democrats; in the other, unwavering Republicans. To address human despoliation of the climate, the

---

It all comes down to the issue of abortion for me. Everything else is second to that.
(Florida)

Democratic family is willing to see its taxes rise, even when that leaves a smaller residue for private purchases. The Republicans feel that the $17,863 now demanded of them is already too high.

The issue isn't whether Republicans are more enthralled by the panoply of products available for sale. They also oppose taxes on moral grounds, underpinned by allusions to individual freedom and limited government. Nor is this to endow Democrats with sainthood. People of all persuasions decide how they want to cast themselves as moral beings. Whether to heed the warnings of scientists—on climate or other topics—can turn on how citizens manage their own balance of entitlements and obligations.

No, Republicans and Democrats don't live in different worlds. They occupy the same social and physical reality. But what they see out there—or choose to—takes different shapes and forms. Nor do we come by all our impressions on our own. Democrats are more apt to accept the interpretations of established research and learning, from the hard sciences through their softer cousins. This is partly because more of them have gone through more years of formal schooling. Even before 2016, Democrats drew more holders of bachelor's and advanced degrees. Yet Republicans can also point to their own catchment of college graduates, including many with professional credentials.

This chapter's consideration of climate and colleges exposes some common themes. One is that Republicans have a greater affinity for business, with its skewed distribution of income, wealth, and profits. So it cannot be said they are opposed to innovation. From robber barons to Silicon Valley, industrial and commercial success has been based on breaking old molds and pioneering new paths. Yet since this is the case, it may be wondered why Republicans are so loath to expand the parameters of marriage or accept sexual experimentation. Beyond the business sphere, Republicans seem more threatened by changes in society. More Democrats have accepted this pace. This isn't to deny that there's reason for disquiet about what may be around the bend. Still, Democrats know a future is coming, and are preparing to be part of it. If anyone—a social scientist?—devises a reliable measure, we will likely find that today's Republicans are angrier and gloomier than Democrats.

You work, you get paid. That's it. (Oklahoma)

26
LETHAL WEAPONS

There is nothing intrinsic in firearms to make them a Republican cause. The coupling had to be cultivated. And as with abortion, the party saw a latent electoral bloc, primed for possible co-option. In 2019, the *New York Times* reported that some 50 million households had one or more guns in their homes.[1] This came to four in every ten families and individuals living on their own, for an aggregate of 400 million such weapons. A CBS survey found that 33 percent of owning households had one, 23 percent had two, while the remaining 43 percent had three or more.[2] Here's how one owner described his arsenal for a Pew Research Report: "I own three firearms: a single-shot bolt action Remington 514.22, a Type 38 Japanese infantry rifle, and a Remington 870 12-gauge pump-action shotgun. I'm considering buying a Ruger 10/22, to use along with my old single-shot .22 on the firing range."[3]

Clearly, firearms have a singular significance for those who own them. Apart from aficionados of vintage cars, it's hard to find another possession that looms so large in lives. Nor is it easy to fathom this passion for something built to be so lethal.

For purposes of this chapter, firearms take three basic forms. First are rifles, usually holding one or two shells, which are mainly used for hunting, at firing ranges, and for shooting at impromptu targets. Next are handguns, almost all of which have repeating capacities. They differ from rifles in that they can be concealed in purses or vehicles or carried on a body. Third are military-style weapons, most of which are called semiautomatic. The "semi" qualifier means a trigger must be pulled each time to insert the next cartridge from a magazine. Even so, an experienced finger on a trigger can spew out thirty bullets per

---

The Republicans are the party that promotes Christian values. (Texas)

minute. Such easily purchased arms have been used to extinguish schoolchildren in Connecticut, clubgoers in Florida, civil servants in California, and worshippers in Pittsburgh and Charleston. The largest massacre, in Las Vegas, was effected by fully automatic weapons, which could not be legally sold but were readily modified at home.

No less an authority than Clarence Thomas, arguably the favorite jurist for many Republicans, took time in a 2015 opinion to report that "roughly five million Americans own AR-style semiautomatic rifles." This weaponry, he added, is mostly kept "for lawful purposes, including self-defense and target shooting." (By 2018, the AR total was nearing eight million.) Thomas felt no need to explain how guns built to mow down wartime combatants might be amenable to defending a home, let alone knocking cans off a fence post. Indeed, a few seconds on a trigger could reduce a target to tatters, render an intruder hard to identify, and leave little of Bambi to mount on a wall.

Not surprisingly, owners have reasons at the ready. Since these are instruments created to kill, arguments are more practiced than those for, say, possessing a piano.

- One is to mount resistance against foreign invaders. Were North Korean troops to land at Puget Sound, armed householders could hold them at bay, if not drive them back into the sea. Another is to ward off oppressive officials, notably from federal agencies, who can harass local customs and choices. An example was a Texas religious sect that fired back at agents surrounding their compound. Some groups have military-style encampments, where they hone the arts of armed defiance.
- Next comes hunting. According to the US Fish and Wildlife Service, this pastime has been on a steady decline. In the past, as many as one in three homes had someone with a permit. Now fewer than half that many do. At last count, only 14 million adults held such licenses. Many rural residents keep firearms for dealing with four-legged predators, which is less hunting than corollary to conducting a business.
- A further reason is assembling a collection. Some people are drawn to exotic cookbooks; others have scores of ceramic frogs. But with guns, it can get a bit macabre. Like the hobbyist who floated a six-figure bid for

---

We need to cut back on immigration and prevent radical Islam from taking over America. (Tennessee)

the weapon that took Trayvon Martin's life. What sets this penchant apart is that the products are made for a singular purpose: to kill or maim living creatures.

- The most frequently given reason for arms at home or on one's person is protection. The best and most succinct statement I've seen is by Joseph Olson, a scholar at the Hamline Law School in Minnesota's Twin Cities: "It's immoral for a society to remove from me my ability to protect myself when it cannot protect me."[4]

This declaration, albeit brief, warrants a close reading. Its first premise is that we are entitled to the expectation that our society, or at least our public agencies, will shield us from crime in its sundry forms. So if authorities can't or won't do this job, citizens should be legally allowed to provide this safety on their own. Professor Olson could tell us that few areas are immune to such incursions. A recent FBI count for one year in Minneapolis and St. Paul recorded 59 murders, 2,998 robberies, and 17,198 burglaries, not to mention others that went unreported or where culprits weren't caught. In an ideal world, law officers would not only apprehend felons, but foil offenses before they get underway, and be so pervasive a presence that would-be miscreants might think twice before they start out. In a word, total protection calls for prior prevention. (As in seeking to forestall terrorist attacks.) Since this isn't happening, Professor Olson holds that householders can justifiably arm themselves.

We have no statistics for instances where armed householders have thwarted intruders or otherwise held them at bay. There are such episodes. Indeed, there's hardly a one that the National Rifle Association doesn't highlight in its publications. In fact, very few are actual break-ins. More typical is a woman who has scared off a bellicose former boyfriend. Who has not feared being accosted on a deserted street or in an ill-lit parking lot? Some Republicans, if not most, want to be free to respond with weapons of their own.

Among our most fraught locales are rural and exurban areas, where drug dependencies reach epidemic proportions. Residences are frequent targets of addicts prowling for anything of value toward their next dose. A West Virginia educator told me that this was why he kept a gun in his home and occasionally in his car. He was asked if he would pull a trigger if he found someone lurking

---

I will never vote for any candidate that supports "woman's right to choose." That phrase denies what's being done: slaughtering human beings! (Ohio)

in his home, given the not-small odds of ending that person's life. First came some murmuring about whether the invader was armed, which may not be easy to detect. In the end, he said he didn't know, and hoped the occasion would not arise. Nor is this a theoretical question. Tens of millions of people, most of them Republicans, keep devices designed for killing in their homes. Given that their main purpose is protection, would they openly say they are ready to fire it at a human being? Yet Republicans—person for person—live in the safest sectors of the nation, far removed from forbidding felonies. More to the point is that Republicans—again more than Democrats—see their country as violent terrain. (Long sentences keep potential perpetrators locked up until their vigor has ebbed.) For many years, the focus was on black marauders, seen as bent on racial revenge. More recently, the spotlight has turned to immigrants, viewed as bringing a ferocity nurtured in their native barrios.

That more women now want to own and carry firearms has presented the party with a dividend. That they are accorded coequal welcomes at gun shows and firing ranges bespeaks updated frontier feminism. It's an elevation of Annie Oakley's "Anything you can do, I can do better!" Since women generally have been migrating away from the GOP, its pro-gun plank hopes to mitigate that loss.

And race patently intrudes where firearms are concerned. For example, insofar as Republicans fret about crime, compounding the fear is that the offender confronting them might be black. A white malefactor might make off with your money. With black miscreants, there is an added dread. It is that they may take another moment to exact retribution for what your people have done to their own. Keeping personal weapons for protection has some similarity with to why plantation owners always had arms at the ready.

All this noted, the precincts where guns are most commonly used are within inner cities. Tragically, young black men deploy them to slaughter one another. Not to mention when stray bullets maim youngsters walking to school or a neighbor by a window. Yet at no point has the GOP urged that urban authorities deal directly with the weapons that are ending so many lives. Significantly, its platforms have never called on cities to ban private arsenals. After all, if guns may be legally seized in Baltimore, the next step could be confiscations in rural Montana.

We should put our country first. (Maryland)

In 2017, the most recent figures at this writing, black Americans lost their lives by firearms at almost twelve times the rate for whites.[5] Overwhelmingly, they were slain by members of their own race and age group. A view of some Republicans, if not openly stated, is that such murders help to make society safer. Here's Michael Nutter, a recent Philadelphia mayor, on what isn't said aloud: "It's one bad black guy who has shot another bad black guy, so one less person to worry about."[6]

In 2017, CBS asked a sample of Americans how they felt about firearms. Partisan lines were pronounced. Close to three-quarters of Republicans—71 percent—viewed possession as a "vital" right, while only 24 percent of Democrats did. Six times as many Republicans said the country would be safer if more citizens had guns, and eight times as many said that the Second Amendment is "part of what makes this country great." Over half of Republicans told CBS that mass shootings "are something we have to accept as part of a free society." So it's not surprising that since 1968, Republican platforms have affirmed the right to "collect, own, and use firearms."[7]

In 2008, the Supreme Court's five Republican members faced a duty call from their party. The District of Columbia had set stringent conditions on the purchase and possession of guns. That local law was contested on the ground that it contravened the Constitution's Second Amendment.

Many people can recite its twenty-seven words by heart: "A well regulated militia being necessary to the security of a free state, the right of the people to keep and bear arms shall not be infringed."

For over a quarter of a century—since Clarence Thomas was named in 1991—Republican justices have understood the parameters of their appointments. The first is to safeguard wealth and profits, as with supporting employers when workers seek recognition or redress. Or allowing corporate largesse to dominate the political arena. But these jurists never forget their compact with their less-affluent adherents. Hence their periodic opinions, which endorse their party's positions in areas like abortion, firearms, and race.

Human differ from other creatures, in that they feel obliged to fabricate prose to justify their actions. Thus if a clinic is closed, words must be crafted claiming that this promotes a larger good. Hence June 2008 saw five Republican justices responding to their party's call on private ownership of lethal weapons.

If we can rid our economy of consumer and corporate taxes, the United States will flourish. (Idaho)

But as noted, it won't do to simply issue a single sentence attesting such possession is permissible. There were twenty-seven crucial words that had to be interpreted. What they intended would decide the status of 400 million firearms.

In *District of Columbia v. Heller*, the majority construed a succinct constitutional provision as bestowing an inherent right that their branch had never once acknowledged in the more than two centuries following the amendment's enactment.

Two issues intersect when judges confront governmental actions regarding guns. The first is that those on federal courts were not elected, in contrast to lawmakers at sundry levels. Republican judges have long held that the decisions they hand down should avoid any inkling of legislating from the bench, let alone hints of judicial activism. Some in the GOP still to point to *Brown v. Board of Education*, which ordered the desegregation of schools, as such overreaching. Today, they decry *Roe v. Wade*, which legalized abortion, as judicial usurpation.

But no such hesitation was shown in 2008, when five Republican justices gave themselves the power to make possessing firearms a broad federal right. If asked, they would weave webs of words to show how *Heller* differs decidedly from *Roe*. At the least, we will be assured that the firearms decision was neither legislative nor activist, but an objective exercise in constitutional interpretation.

So to the second issue. It is how best to interpret, and then apply, the language of a law or the Constitution itself. From time to time, members of the Supreme Court feel called upon to wax philosophical. Hence their insistence that they don't just assess each case on its discrete merits, but that consistent principles inspire their opinions.

Republicans generally choose one of two precepts. When it suits them, the preferred tenet is to discern the *plain meaning* of crucial words in a law or provision. Like the unadorned message in "interstate commerce" or "excessive bail." Here the judge is a consummate logician, expert at parsing abstruse sentences. Unfortunately, this principle can't work with the Second Amendment. The problem is the first thirteen of its twenty-seven words.

The allusion to "a well regulated militia" was an explicit qualifier to any right to "bear and keep arms." It might well have allowed firearms only to

---

I'm against political correctness. (Ohio)

members of militias, what today we call the National Guard. The muskets in question could be their own, or supplied by the government and stored at home.

A plain-meaning analysis must take in all twenty-seven words, not just the final fourteen. So with the Second Amendment, its militia allusion precludes a plain-meaning reading that would yield a Republican result.

Hence recourse to a different doctrine, one its adherents call "originalism." Here judges go back to the time when a law was enacted or a constitutional provision was written. Here the focus is on the *intent* of the original figures who chose the words or contributed to their enactment. With more recent legislation, there can be recourse to several sources, like committee hearings and reports or statements during debates. But with the Constitution, its authors are long dead. Still, we have James Madison's notes of the drafters' 1787 deliberations, as well as *The Federalist Papers* and state ratifying conventions, plus historical records on what life was like in those days. So parsing sentences is not enough. Research may be needed to fathom how the keeping and bearing of firearms was originally construed in 1791, when the Second Amendment was adopted.

It fell to Antonin Scalia to write on his own behalf and for his four fellow Republicans. It ran to sixty-four pages, for a total of 21,410 words. That length was deemed necessary, because it was an excursion into colonial history, endeavoring to re-create how people must have felt about guns. Scalia may have sent his clerks to pore over yellowed documents, as well as citations in briefs that were friendly to his side. A sampling of what was found is below.

What Scalia produced was akin to the term paper of a sedulous student. His opinion was replete with citations, chosen to prompt an inference that owning and carrying of guns was common in the 1700s, often with official sanction. He then seeks to persuade his readers that they must mirror the mind-set of James Madison, the original author of the amendment, and the legislators who added it to the Constitution.

This recourse was necessary because a plain-meaning explication would have had to address the militia preface. Hence the switch to originalist suppositions. Not to mention the premise that nouns and verbs quill-penned in the 1700s of slaveholders and chimney pieces must control how lives are led in the 2000s.

Republicans come from many backgrounds, but we are united by our desires for responsible leadership, limited government, and free markets. (Texas)

> "Hath not every Subject power to keep Arms, as well as Servants in his House for defence of his Person?" *A Complete Collection of State-Tryals* (1719)
>
> "Free Negros, Mulattos, or Indians, and Owners of Slaves, seated at Frontier Plantations, may obtain Licence from a Justice of Peace, for keeping, Arms, &c." *A Collection of All the Acts of Assembly Now in Force, in the Colony of Virginia* (1733)
>
> "Yet a Person might keep Arms in his House, or on his Estate, on the Account of Hunting, Navigation, Travelling, and on the Score of Selling them in the way of Trade or Commerce, or such Arms as accrued to him by way of Inheritance." *A New Pandect of Roman Civil Law* (1734)
>
> "What law forbids the veriest pauper, if he can raise a sum sufficient for the purchase of it, from mounting his Gun on his Chimney Piece?" *Some Considerations on the Game Laws* (1796)

The five Republican justices knew what their party expected of them. It was to decide for the plaintiff, Dick Heller, and their partisans, who feel passionately about their guns.

Government should be small and our military should be strong. (Arizona)

FORTRESS AMERICA

While making notes on how Republicans react to the rest of the world, I found myself amid a welter of slogans, pronouncements, and exhortations. Here are some.

Isolationist	*America First*
The War Party	*Fortress America*
Make America Great Again	*Collective Security*
Nation Building	*Beacon for the World*
Containing Communism	*Leader of the Free World*
Über Alles	*L'Amour de la Patrie*
USA! USA!	*Great Plains Pacifism*
Boots on the Ground	*Fire and Fury*
City on a Hill	*Flags in Lapels*

The Civil War, the nation's bloodiest, and which was formally against another nation, occurred during the Republicans' first administration. Yet it would be incorrect to say that the party started that conflict. Its impetus came early in 1861, when several Southern states seceded to form the Confederate States of America, a self-proclaimed sovereign nation. By now historians agree that war was bound to ensue. But that only commenced when Confederate troops lay siege to a Union fort in South Carolina. It was a provocation akin to Pearl Harbor. Once Southerners opened fire, the North had no choice but to reply in kind.

The media overcovers the GOP and gives Democrats a free ride. (Virginia)

It was in 1898, a generation after the Civil War, that the GOP showed its spurs as a war party. The administration headed by William McKinley and Theodore Roosevelt contrived pretexts to invade and commandeer the Spanish colony of Cuba. If that island was only ninety miles from Florida, combat soon crossed the Pacific to the Philippines. Easy victories brought these provinces and Puerto Rico under American dominion. For Republicans, it was a model.

So perhaps it was not surprising that when the *Lusitania* was torpedoed in 1917, joining a European war had broad Republican support. The next year saw hostilities ending and Republicans taking control of the Senate. It soon became evident that dealing with peace would be another matter. The Treaty of Versailles, essentially a postwar charter, was submitted to the upper chamber, where it was summarily rebuffed. The chief reason given was that the accord would require the United States to join an international body called the League of Nations. Republican senators voted 28–12 for rejection. (Democrats backed it, but only by two votes.)[1] The GOP margin against a multinational undertaking portended a posture that remains strong today.

During the next two decades, Republicans embraced a position then called "isolationism." Most simply, it called for curbing involvements with other countries. It was redolent of Thomas Jefferson's paradigm:

I am for free commerce with all nations; political connections with none.
I am opposed to a standing army and a navy, which by the eternal wars in which they will implicate us, will sink us underneath them.[2]

These principles were put in practice during the 1920s. Yet in the first year of the next decade, even Jefferson's "free commerce" exception was jettisoned. A Republican-controlled House of Representatives passed the Smoot-Hawley Tariff Act by a crushing 244–12 vote. Both parties agreed to cut military budgets, even aware of bellicosity in Europe and the Far East. The view was that if others chose to fool with fire, we weren't playing that game.

The 1930s were also the decade of redoubtable Republicans, like George Norris of Nebraska, William Borah of Idaho, and South Dakota's Gerald Nye. Their isolationism was more than geopolitical, since it added a pacifist underpinning. Nye went further, contending that the munitions industry made its

---

The GOP stands for pro-life, school choice, and less taxes. (Arizona)

profits by fomenting slaughter. A sharp test came early in 1941, with World War II persisting in Europe, and Germany seeming likely to vanquish Great Britain. President Roosevelt asked Congress to approve sending military supplies to Britain. Republicans in the House of Representatives voted 135–24 against it. The party preferred to sit out that conflict.

The United States never formally decided to join World War II, but its entry was forced by Japan's attack on Pearl Harbor. Poignantly, it was not unlike Fort Sumter, eighty years earlier. Another similarity was that both the Confederates and the Japanese were confident they could defeat a larger industrial power.

When the United Nations was established at the war's conclusion in 1945, Republican senators voted 23–6 to join. Four years later, the North Atlantic Treaty Organization was put in place to face a looming Soviet Union. Republican senators signed on 33–11. What propelled the NATO alliance was Soviet expansion: a vast military threat, underscored by a militant ideology. These voting margins signaled an internationalist turning by the party. Or at least a variant termed "collective security," conceding a need to collaborate with other countries. Left for the future would be how far the party would stay in pacts based on parity of partners.

Republican secretaries of state, from John Foster Dulles under Dwight Eisenhower to Richard Nixon's Henry Kissinger, promoted an unalloyed internationalist stance. More than that, the United States was to be the preeminent player in alliances across the globe. By United Nations counts, most of the nations in the world would acknowledge the United States as the leader of the free world.

Nor was this a rotating position, with other countries having a turn. The era was to be the American Century. This epithet was coined by Henry Luce, the paramount media magnate of that time and an éminence grise of the GOP. It was to be a span starting in June 1944, on D-Day of World War II, and lasting at least to 2044, if not an infinite future. And leadership is not just heading the pack. It requires the concurrence of followers, ensuring a consensus in a common cause.

Republicans accepted this mantle through the administration of George H. W. Bush, who enlisted a mélange of allies for his first foray against Iraq.

I'm tired of the government poking holes in my ship to help raise others, when I'm doing all the work. (Alabama)

The Cold War lasted forty-five years. It began with Winston Churchill's 1946 "Iron Curtain" speech at a Missouri college and ended with the Soviet Union's implosion and dissolution in 1991. The chief protagonists were the US and the USSR, China also figuring on and off as an ally of the latter, since they shared Marxian antecedents. Yet the entire forty-five years never saw a physical skirmish between the two principal protagonists, let alone nuclear launches. Nor was this restraint fortuitous. Leaders on both sides, including successive Republicans, strove to keep communications and negotiations open.

Instead, the United States went to war with countries that were seen as Soviet allies. The most notable were North Korea and North Vietnam, the latter allied with informal forces in South Vietnam. Altogether, 94,736 Americans perished in these two incursions, which were orchestrated by administrations of both parties.

Even when Democrats were at the helm, Republicans gave these forays unalloyed support. Republican reasoning was simple. These wars were necessary to confront the menace of global communism. And if much of the Vietnam intervention occurred during Lyndon Johnson's presidency, Republicans were its most stalwart supporters. Hence GOP disgust at anti-war sentiment, seen as disloyal when not cowardly, and which never emerged in its own ranks. Those with lukewarm feelings, or who opposed war altogether, were branded as short on national loyalty. Even now, with almost a half-century for reflection, few in the GOP cast Vietnam as a defeat or concede the incursion was a mistake.

Since at least September 11, 2001, Republicans have viewed some or most components of the Islamic world as analogous to the Soviet challenge. Even so, they are a wholly different kind of foe. Instead of deploying infantry divisions and nuclear arsenals, they use surprise suicide missions. Indeed, all that's needed are a handful of zealots willing to die. Hence a tendency to call them terrorists. The dread they evoke is not of mass destruction by warheads. It is localized and seemingly random, as happened with the ending of 2,606 lives in New York City. Manchester, Paris, Nice, Madrid, and Nairobi have all had their turn. The aim is to demoralize, to keep millions of people perpetually anxious lest they be next. No one knows if or when or where a tower or theater or train will be targeted.

I like the Republican Party due to Abraham Lincoln, who was its founder. (Indiana)

Republicans haven't a common stance on these new kinds of combatants. As of this writing, none have spoken of overrunning Iran, as it was accepted as necessary in Iraq. At this point, few if any Republicans are happy about maintaining a military presence in Syria, Afghanistan, or Islamic regions in Africa. Still, contingencies can be surmised from the past. If overseas hostilities are commenced and American lives begin to be lost, Republicans will rally round to show loyalty to the troops on the ground. Doubters will be cast as disloyal, as will putative allies who decline to support the incursion. In all, the party of patriotism is rarely heard asserting an ongoing war is wrong.

Yet it's also plain that Islamic enmity is not going to go away. Thus far, the most palpable Republican strategy is to prevent more Muslims from entering the country and keep a vigilant eye on those already here. In our adversaries' own terms, they are engaged in a "holy war," a cause dedicated to rooting out secular impurities and perversions.

Yet there's a marked asymmetry here. The United States' reactions to Islam have no hallowed foundations. In confronting the Soviet Union, capitalist and constitutional freedoms were seen to be at stake. The United States does not have an ideological animus toward Islam to match the fervor of jihadist sects. Even purblind patriots have no riposte to shouts of "Death to America!" heard in Middle Eastern streets. The chief response to terrorist acts is to keep them from recurring.

There's more to the asymmetry. There's also an imbalance at ground level. With drones and missiles now on the menu, uniformed personnel can be thousands of miles from enemy lines. Those seen as our foes can draw on millions of young people, ready to give their lives and often avid for that chance. As is all too evident, a single suicide warrior can inflict massive damage, by a repeating weapon, commandeering a vehicle, or wearing an explosives vest. Thus far the Republican response has been to provide arms to allies and have Iraqis, Afghans, and Syrians do most of the fighting for us.

Democrats had always been more unabashedly internationalist. Most recently, they took this path by championing the North American Free Trade Agreement, the Trans-Pacific Partnership, and the Paris Climate Accord. Donald Trump's antipathy to such pacts was long clear for anyone who had been watching or cared. But his was a presidency no one ever expected to see.

Democrats are bad on First and Second Amendment rights. (Kentucky)

That noted, it was also evident by 2017 that a strong majority of Republicans were more than willing to support whatever stance he chose. Nor is it true to say that members of Congress were cowed by his bullying demeanor. They, and others who willingly joined the executive branch, had been ready to discard the courting and compromise inherent in multination compacts, or accepting allies as equals.

Instead, the party is reconceiving the rubrics of Fortress America and America First. Under these dicta, the nation can still be a global power, but on its own, without allies or alliances. It is a momentous undertaking, with the world watching to see how far this stance will secure the ends it seeks.

A war party? The record has been mixed. As the earlier recounting showed, World War I and World War II both began and ended under Democratic administrations. The Korean war started with an invasion from the collectivist Northern segment of that country. US forces, following a decision by Harry Truman, intervened to repel the incursion. This was in fact achieved, with no small loss of life, and was quickly concluded by Dwight Eisenhower. Vietnam had a not dissimilar North-South scenario. The United States had a lengthy history of militancy, from Eisenhower's providing so-called advisers at the outset, to escalations by Kennedy, Johnson, and Nixon. It ended in an American defeat, albeit without a formal surrender. Some Republicans place the onus on disloyal protestors at home. Others have refused to call it that, intimating that the United States does not lose wars.

The two Iraq involvements were conceived by Republicans, both named George Bush. The first was limited and sagely enlisted allies. As such, it was a small exercise in collective security. The second Iraq incursion was essentially a solo act, which ended by devastating an entire region. It was the first fully Republican war since the Spanish-American foray. This seismic shift came with the advent of the second George Bush, who had neither grounding nor aptitude for foreign dealings. Two counselors, Richard Cheney and Paul Wolfowitz, persuaded him to ignore putative allies and plunge into Iraq. This launched a go-it-alone posture for the GOP. It was not strictly isolationist, since American troops would be surging into the Middle East. But it was literally an isolated undertaking, in that not more than a token effort was made to enlist allies.

I cannot abide the constant march toward totalitarian socialism. (Kansas)

Donald Trump's administration has preserved this posture. One of its first acts was to become the one nation out of 198 to reject the Paris Climate Accord. Not long after, perhaps to preserve that distinction, it was one of two dissents of 193 votes on a United Nations resolution condemning Cuba. (Only Israel pitched in to help.)

Nor were these simply the penchants of an idiosyncratic president. No Republican voices were heard disputing this kind of defiance, nor even chagrin about being out of step. In the nuclear arena, the administration acted alone in seeking to isolate Iran, in trying to parlay with North Korea, and in abrogating an arms agreement with Russia. Here again, a deep GOP silence signaled acquiescence on these and other fronts. Not least was going along with an aggressive tariff war, unlike any since Smoot-Hawley. Nor have elected officials posed alternatives to going solo. It may be that a party centered in Oklahoma and Idaho has little inherent interest in international matters. Either way, a hush is the party's voice on foreign affairs.

Donald Trump's "America First" may have started as a slogan, but it has become more than that. As he has averred, all independent nations give priority to their own interests. This also holds among those who usually turn to cooperation and collaboration. Even so, Republican views of sovereignty differ sharply from conceptions found elsewhere. (There was a facsimile in British voters who supported withdrawing from the European Union.) Still, "America First" lacks specificity. After all, Danes and Dutch people could argue that they serve their countries best by acting in concert with allies and neighbors.

Arguably, a better epithet for the emerging GOP would be "Fortress America," a term long out of use, but which is nonetheless apposite. Once realized, here's what it might entail. The nation would have a robust military, undergirded by state-of-the-art armaments. Despite Republican antipathy to taxes, they seldom scant that branch. In this, they would rally behind Alexander Hamilton: "I acknowledge my aversion to every project that is calculated to disarm the government of a single weapon which in any possible contingency might be usefully employed for the general defense and security."[3]

These words could be in a Republican platform today, especially in a refusal to settle for anything short of an absolute pledge to defense and security. It invokes images of a continental citadel. Its hallmarks would be impenetrable

---

Republican policies lead to free market competition in health care. (Florida)

borders and fortified coastlines, akin to castles of yore, with modern versions of rugged drawbridges and murky moats. A start would be to erect a high fortified wall, straddling the 1,993 miles of the US-Mexican border. As needs no recounting, such a project figured prominently in Trump's 2016 campaign. ("And Mexico will pay for it!") Once he was in office, it was given priority as a pledge to be filled. Nor was this simply one president's cenotaph to himself. It became the party's cause as well. When he unilaterally finessed funds for the fence, 227 of the party's 252 lawmakers backed his arrogation. (That's a round 90 percent.) Indeed, it could be seen as a first installment for the physical face of Fortress America. True, it was not an updated Maginot Line, designed to thwart enemy troops. Rather, its aim was to keep out menacing civilians from Mexico and Central and South America, plus terrorists posing as refugees. So along with preserving the nation's racial balance, a wall was also an arm of foreign policy.

Equally crucial are airborne weapons, often in remote locations, capable of lashing out across the globe. Nations like North Korea and Iran would presumably flinch and cower, knowing they could be turned to ashes from afar. So this balustrade is not simply defensive. It will be ready to send assaults anywhere on the planet. Given the ambit of this scenario, the term "isolationist" hardly seems to apply. But whether fantasy or policy, it is a current GOP vision for American supremacy.

And who is to do the fighting? Since the most bellicose Republicans are at least middle-aged, it will fall to younger generations to face mutilation and death. (A survey of Republicans in Congress found just one with an offspring in uniform.) Conscription was ended following defeat in Vietnam, so the military now functions with volunteers. Officers have mainly gone to modest colleges; only a fifth attended the services' academies. Enlisted personnel are almost wholly working class, with a disproportion of recruits from Republican strongholds. More precisely, states ranking highest in enlistments average eight points higher in GOP turnouts. It's likely that most of these young warriors signed up with the approval of Republican parents.

A small but significant Republican constituency is the professional officer corps. Not surprisingly, whether fledgling cadets or starred generals, they properly maintain political silence. One study found that most of those who vote

---

I don't believe we can improve lives by yelling hate and adding more laws.
(California)

don't register with a party, which is what one would hope and expect. But of those who do, they sign up as Republican by a four-to-one margin.

This makes sense, if only because the GOP is the more martial party. There may be another cause: the military's demographics. Rural America, especially the South and the Midwest, has long honored careers at arms. Most officers now come through ROTC programs at land-grant colleges, like Purdue and Texas A&M. Indeed, a commission usually brings upward mobility. Almost all our generals and admirals rose from modest origins.

There can be no doubt that Republicans want their nation to be *great*, with such stature ranking high in their catechism of desires. This standing is ordinarily construed in military and economic terms. (The party has scant interest in esteem allied with science or the arts.) Nor is it moral stature, as with societies known for treating people fairly or taking in refugees. Rather, its fulcrum is unrivaled power—military and economic—mighty enough to make the rest of the globe tremble. When Republicans travel abroad, they want to encounter deference, a grounded recognition of America's renown. In a word, the "Great" on the campaign caps is meant to be read as "The Greatest."

It's not likely many Republicans would want their country to attain anything less than undisputed primacy. But if this is to be the goal of foreign relations, it remains to ask what measures will be required. In the economic sphere, the GOP answer is simple. If businesses are exempted from burdensome barriers and allowed to freely pursue profits, America will mount an economy unparalleled in the world.

As a corollary to patriotism, Republicans hold that the United States is by far the *finest* country on the globe, by whatever measures are employed or aggregated. They will argue that its people enjoy more personal and civic freedom, wider opportunity, and a higher living standard. Nor is this a debate to be cluttered with studies or statistics, let alone scholarly research. The party's evidence is that so many people clamor to come here, by whatever means they can.

A kindred Republican penchant is to deny any notion that other nations may conduct their affairs more equitably or rationally than the United States. As in looking at how France provides health care, or Belgium curbs fossil fuels,

---

I want government to stay out of my life. (Georgia)

or Australia addresses firearms. Or why Japan ranks low on homicides, Canada imprisons fewer of its residents, and Dutch teenagers seldom get pregnant. Findings like these never obscure Republican position papers. Since the United States stands first, it cannot admit it might learn from—let alone emulate or admire—the experience or attainments of others.

For many Republicans, foreign interventions are explained as unadorned realism. Two presidents named George Bush sent troops to the Middle East for the same reason that Ronald Reagan deployed them in Grenada and Lebanon. A power with global pretensions has interests on every continent. Therefore, threats to the nation's security can arise anywhere. True, the Korean and Vietnam incursions were given an ideological dressing, since the adversaries held to collectivist tenets. But few argued that the United States intervened to bring those countries the blessings of free enterprise. More recently, conflicts with Iraq, Afghanistan, and Syria have been conducted solely as military operations. No talk is heard about how the United States offers an alternative to Islam. True, too, there came murmurings about bringing democracy to Iraq. But as Britain showed the world in earlier times, honorable ambitions are preceded by gunboats.

This noted, there are still Republicans who believe that their country has a special calling. In their view, this nation has been chosen to act as a model for the world. Hence Alexander Hamilton's exhortation to its fledgling citizens: "It belongs to us to vindicate the honor of the human race."[4] This dictum holds that all people everywhere need tutelage in American ways. For a while, this was called "nation building," with the United States as the exemplar and architect. For a while, experts presumed adept in that sphere accompanied each incursion. Nor was this purblind arrogance. The templates were the rebuilding of Japan and Germany in the aftermath of World War II.

Currently, few elected Republicans feel obliged to remodel other nations. If Alexander Hamilton has modern heirs, they are managers of global corporations who seek amenable conditions for conducting their enterprises. Chief executive officers earnestly believe that what they produce will elevate the world. Taken together, Coca-Cola and Boeing, Disney and Google, Facebook and ExxonMobil infuse American ways across borders. That they are embraced

---

The Republican Party is the party of Ronald Reagan. It cares more about ensuring that America and her values are protected and preserved. (Wisconsin)

voluntarily attests to their appeal, not imperialist duress. Even amid nativism and populism, corporate resources have a crucial role in maintaining Republican sway. Their quest for profits, increasingly earned abroad, will ensure an international thrust for the party.

I don't agree with spreading the wealth to lazy assholes. (Oregon)

28
THREE LIES

Eleven years ago, Megan McArdle wrote an essay called "The Politics of Prevarication." It was about Republicans' efforts to undercut Barack Obama's health-care plan.[1] Her analysis deserves updating. Since that time, Republicans have elevated lying to an art form. In fact, this tactic got underway well before the advent of Donald Trump.

Republican legislators, in particular, have perfected what I like to call "bare-faced lies." They are uttered without diffidence or apology; indeed, with no disposition to offer reasoning or evidence. Indeed, there's no care if it's generally realized that what is being said isn't true. Their purpose is to exercise their power as they wish, deploying a few fictions as window dressing.

Three such prevarications will be considered on the pages ahead. One is that the nation is under siege by a surge of "voter fraud." Another is that Republicans are sedulously dedicated to "women's health." The third is that the party is committed to creating "well-paying jobs."

Voter Fraud. Since at least 2011, the GOP has made resolute efforts to truncate the nation's electorate. This can only be seen as purposeful reversal. Until recently, the nation has successively widened the franchise. Barriers based on gender, race, and age have all been altered or eliminated, with the last lowered from twenty-one to eighteen. Even literacy tests were proscribed.

Republicans have never been happy with these trends. Indeed, there's a very basic reason: many don't regard access to the ballot as a universal right. In fact, strictly speaking, they don't see it as a right at all. Thus they can see situations where it could be reasonably suspended or denied, much like a driver's license.

I believe police officers should get the benefit of the doubt. (California)

151

The most striking example is denying the vote to inmates and persons on probation or parole, which in some states continues for the remainder of their lives. What this says is that the franchise must be earned, which most citizens do by steering clear of crime. According to the Sentencing Project, fully six million Americans have had felony convictions.[2] In states like Mississippi and Kentucky, it's one of every eleven of their adult residents.

At the same time, there's a concurrent feeling that felons should be able to regain their vote after they have, as the phrase goes, paid their debt to society. In 2018, Florida held a referendum on restoring votes to former felons. A poll found 87 percent of Democrats favoring the measure. The general view was that Republicans would object. Yet as a surprise to some observers, fully 52 percent of them voted for it, which ensured its passage. (Shortly thereafter, the state's Republican legislators undercut the public vote. It decreed that all former felons must pay back long-dormant court costs if they wanted the ballot.)

The last few decades have seen a spate of activity by Republican legislatures. One tactic is to set onerous obstacles for new voters who seek to join the rolls. Another enables the removal of persons already on the books, if they move or change their names or miss an interim election. Only afterward do they learn that their votes will no longer be counted or recorded. Such moves were initiated in Ohio, and were obligingly upheld by the Supreme Court's five Republican members.[3] States where the party holds control have also reduced the number of polling places and cut back on opportunities for early voting. Predictably, such measures are applied most sedulously in districts with palpable Democratic margins.

But the most common tactic in Republican states has been to require that everyone seeking to vote must produce a government-issued document with an embedded photograph. A driver's license will suffice, as would a passport or a gun permit. Expressly *not* allowed are cards issued to students by state colleges or persons receiving food stamps. These omissions were not accidental. Those excluded are less prone to vote Republican; firearms owners are less apt to be Democrats.

Given our automotive age, most adults do possess a current driver's license. But a lot of people don't. A 2016 study, based on US Department of Transportation records, found that 14 percent of Georgia's adults didn't have

---

I do not support homosexuality or abortion as birth control. (North Carolina)

one, nor did 18 percent in Oklahoma. In actual numbers, 1,993,107 Texans of voting age were in this category. A Department of Justice survey found that black residents of Louisiana were four times less apt than whites to have official documents with a photograph. And a University of Wisconsin study revealed that while 53 percent of black adults in Milwaukee didn't have drivers' licenses, this was so for only 15 percent of white adults elsewhere in the state.[4] For voting to be a basic right, it must remain readily available. Demanding a license gravely undermines the concept of citizenship.

Of course, the legislators weren't stupid. They allowed states to issue, on request, an alternative document. For this, though, one had to personally journey to a Motor Vehicles office, have your photograph taken, and fill out a lengthy form. In Wisconsin, to cite one state, you had to specify your hair color, height, and Social Security number. A fee was ordinarily charged. It could be waived, though only after proving that their incomes were below the poverty line, which means bringing in a batch of papers. All this was not for clearance to drive a school bus or an interstate truck. It was to be permitted to vote. (Nor was it clear what provision was made for housebound elders or patients in nursing homes.) Thus far, no states have made public—at least not on available websites—how many proxy cards have been requested or issued.

Since this requirement would be burdensome for a not-small pool of citizens, its Republican sponsors have felt it prudent to fashion a justification. The rationale for demanding an official card, they averred, was to thwart voter fraud. Thus the party framed an account pronouncing that elections across the country are routinely abused by men and women who vote under bogus names or addresses, or by using other people's identities. Here they were abetted by their president, who claimed he came second in the popular count because several million people had illegally voted for his opponent. Having to present an official document with your likeness would prevent such deceptions. It's how we keep hijackers from boarding airplanes.

The first step, taken in May 2017, was to create a Presidential Advisory Commission on Election Integrity, to be chaired by the vice president. Almost its first move was to send an ultimatum to all states, demanding that they provide full access to their electoral registers, including Social Security digits. (No fewer than 136,787,187 people voted in 2016.) The purported aim of this

We hear every day about bizarre trends like suspending students for wearing the American flag on their T-shirts. (Georgia)

massive inquiry was to unveil any miscreants who might have voted concurrently in several states.

Needless to say, states with Democratic administrations balked. But the most prominent refusal came from the elected secretary of state in Mississippi, long a Republican redoubt. "They can go jump in the Gulf of Mexico," he proclaimed, citing his obligation to "protect the privacy of our citizens."

Clearly, the commission had bitten off more than it could chew, let alone what it could digest. In January 2018, after a lifespan of 231 days, it dissolved and turned the issue of election integrity over to the Departments of Justice and, ominously, Homeland Security.

Still, the specter of voter fraud has not been allowed to die. Instead, the commission's chores were farmed out to the Heritage Foundation, a tax-exempt think tank in large part funded by the Koch brothers. Its principal project has been to devise a Voter Fraud Database. In its first report, its analysts found 1,132 "proven instances of voter fraud," arrayed along a time line with the first case in 1948. All the states had at least one offense, ranging from 14 in Alabama to 123 in Minnesota.

Whether 1,132 is a lot or a little, or just the tip of an iceberg, is a judgment call. What we do know is that a total of 972,912,497 votes were cast in the nine biennial elections from 2000 through 2016. If all the frauds were in that span—in fact, many were much earlier—the 1,132 came to one of every 859,463 of the ballots recorded in this period. And this ratio doesn't include primaries or odd-numbered years, which would easily raise it to one in over a million.

The Brennan Center at New York University, another tax-exempt body, decided to give the Heritage research a close look. To start, it found that only 488 of the 1,132 cases occurred in the last ten years. So over half were more than a decade in the past, including the one in 1948. The Brennan analysts focused on offenses that photo identification cards are intended to address. It found that only ten of the 1,132 involved "impersonation fraud" where an individual signed in to vote using someone else's name. Some of these were apparently caught before identity cards were used. Still, it can be agreed that the impersonators—all ten of them—would be more readily snared if they

---

I believe in the death penalty as a method to stop killing. (Oregon)

showed a card with the wrong name or photograph. Using the 2000–2016 voter roll, ten work out to one in each 97,291,250 ballots.[5]

The Heritage researchers also looked for instances where noncitizens voted. Here it did better, coming up with forty-one cases. One, from Texas, shows how severe the retribution can be. Rosa Maria Ortega, a noncitizen, was found guilty on two counts of voter fraud for voting in the November 2012 general election and at the 2014 primary. Ortega claimed she thought she was a citizen, and blamed her lack of education for the mix-up. But prosecutors pointed out that Ortega had previously noted that she was a non-citizen when applying for a driver's license. A judge sentenced her to eight years' imprisonment, after which she faces the possibility of deportation.

Would requiring a driver's license for voting have caught or deterred the forty-one noncitizens? As it happens, foreigners can and do obtain this document. An Australian corporation may send a team of engineers to Idaho for a six-month assignment. Idaho will be pleased to grant them licenses on the same basis as domestic applicants. Nor will that document attest whether they are US citizens.

Another 174 cases—with 114 of them in Minnesota—could arguably be called fraud. In these instances, persons arriving to vote were truthful about their age, their citizenship, and their place of residence. But all had criminal records. Some didn't realize that this disqualified them. Some others did and tried to vote anyway. Most never had their ballots recorded. All in all, the great majority of the 1,132 Heritage cases were not ballots that were illegally cast. They run a huge gamut, from charges of illicit assistance and irregular petition signing to outdated home addresses and improper interventions by election officials.

But then, Republicans have known all along that fraud has never been a problem, certainly not in the last half century. Their aim is not to thwart dishonest voting, but to keep certain groups of citizens from voting at all.

Women's Health. A Republican goal has been that abortions should no longer be available in the United States. This pursuit has been extremely effective in buttressing its base. Not least, it has cemented an alliance between ardent Roman Catholics and evangelical congregations, who in earlier times were

---

I dislike big government. It's interfering with my rights. (Alabama)

rancorous adversaries. The sects now join in championing "the unborn" and "right to life," attesting to their conviction that human existence begins at conception.

By far the most effective of the Republicans' tactics has been to force the closing of clinics where most abortion procedures occur. The great majority of these procedures are medically or surgically simple, and thus do not require hospital equipment or facilities. Hence the advent of freestanding centers, which usually offer an array of services, including prenatal tests and cancer screening. Planned Parenthood is the best known of such centers, and therefore a principal target.

Republican legislators habitually decry rules and regulations issued by government agencies, claiming that they stifle innovation, diminish profits, and are always burdensome. But when it comes to the above-mentioned clinics, animosity to interference is set aside. By now, antiabortion statutes are familiar. They require that clinics maintain the costly appurtenances of a hospital, such as surgical suites equipped for gastric bypasses or liver transplants. There are also provisos specifying widths of corridors, inventories of pharmaceuticals, even spaces for parking. The real aim, of course, is to impose enormous expenses of installation and upkeep on clinics, which their revenues cannot possibly cover.

Another hurdle is to require that all physicians who practice at clinics to have admitting privileges at nearby hospitals. Republican lawmakers are well aware that few hospitals will oblige, largely because they would rather not be identified with a controversial procedure. In truth, these rules have no rational purpose. If problems arise at a clinic—which is extremely rare—the patient can be sped to the nearest emergency room. In such situations, patients are treated immediately, without being asked if they had been referred by a privilege-carrying physician.

So here we have yet another Republican lie. It is their claim that all these directives betoken their solicitude for the health and safety of the women who arrive. The party has never been notably concerned with matters of health or safety. Its position is that citizens should purchase whatever care they choose from private providers. Nor is it particularly supportive of the women who rely

---

Racial quotas and affirmative action do a lot of harm for minorities. They don't need these "programs." (New York)

on clinics, especially if they have been sexually active without the sacrament of marriage.

These laws have worked. Kentucky once had seventeen clinics offering the procedure. By 2017, fully sixteen of them had closed, not voluntarily, but due to the mounting costs of widening corridors and stockpiling drugs that were never used. How far Republicans care about women's health was bared in a federal courtroom in 2016. During an interchange, Texas's attorney general was asked what recourse there would be for women in his state if all of its remaining clinics closed because of the prohibitive costs of complying with these and other rules. He replied that they could journey across the border to adjacent New Mexico. But that state, he was reminded, didn't mandate high-tech surgical suites, ostensibly to protect patients' health. Was he counseling women to use facilities that were ostensibly less safe? Texas's chief law officer did not offer an answer.

Republican strategy is also revealed by its position on Planned Parenthood. That philanthropy was founded almost a century ago, by patrician Republicans, who viewed its services as an extension of social work. (The family of both Bush presidents was particularly committed.) Adhering to that tradition, its clinics offer a wide range of services dedicated to women's health and infant safety, like prenatal counseling. Abortion is only one of many of its services, and not the most common. But because that choice is offered, the GOP has cast Planned Parenthood as totally tainted and would deny public funding to any and all of its activities.

High Wages. A Republican mantra is that only its precepts will free the economy to generate decent jobs with generous paychecks. In the party's formulary, if employers are fully free to pursue profits, they will be able to create well-paying positions. Capitalism, so conceived, is a win-win algorithm. Of course, successful owners and investors usually amass great wealth. But the entire nation also benefits from enjoying new products and expanded spending power. Republican economics accepts that there will be income disparities. But that is part of its everyone-wins equation. If all are to prosper, the truly talented must have a prospect of being rewarded. Hence too the party's aversion to taxing the

---

I believe in accepting immigrants who share our values and will assimilate quickly.
(North Carolina)

well-to-do. Here the hypothesis is that the more they are allowed to keep, the more will be invested in better jobs for everyone.

In fact, things aren't going well with wages, at least for median Americans. For those at or close to the middle of the pyramid, the story is one of stagnation.

Here's a snapshot of men in the workforce. In 2017, the most recent figures at this writing, a man at the wage-and-salary midpoint ended the year with earnings of $46,741. Yet this has barely budged from a generation earlier, when in today's dollars, the 1973 median was $43,981. By contrast, things were very different in the prior quarter-century. From 1947 through 1972, men's paychecks almost doubled, rising by 90 percent.

If seems safe to say that most workers would welcome higher pay, either in jobs they now have or to which they might move. However, there's a catch here. It is that holding out the promise of high wages runs contrary to a basic capitalist concept. Here's what I recall from Economics 102: employers offer as little as they need to, to recruit and retain workers with the qualities the jobs require.

This dictum applies from part-time servers at Burger King all the way to a pop star negotiating a multimillion-dollar tour. Simply stated, employers do not pay a dime more than they need to, which is why Republicans oppose labor unions, minimum-wage legislation, and benefits and pensions. The less paid to workers, the more can be allocated to for owners' dividends and executive largesse. (Indeed, top management is one sphere where they to give themselves more than they would be paid if they tried to sell their talents in an open market.)

Hence all the resources deployed to eviscerate unions. In living memory, it is all but impossible to find a Republican platform or pronouncement that has supported unions in any form. (Even for police officers or immigration agents.) After all, collective bargaining can press employers to pay more than they would otherwise have to. If workers are forced on their own, it's easier to address them singly and present them with the lowest possible wage. Employers also prefer having a surfeit of persons with the traits and skills they need. The larger the pool of applicants, the more desperate they will be and willing to settle for smaller checks. A recent example: the mantra that every high school

---

With stricter gun control, criminals will still have access to them, which puts all American citizens' safety at risk. (Alabama)

student in the country should be required to learn computer coding. The reason is not, as is usually said, to attune them to the coming century's careers. Rather, it accords with the Republican's low-wage imperative. The more people who become skilled in software, the larger the catchment of candidates, and the less you have to pay them.

So workers who aspire to higher pay are being bamboozled by the GOP, whose business arm has no wish to add even an extra dime. Given its desire to depress wages, it is appropriate to wonder how far the party wants to take that aim. Will it extend to reducing the compensation, say, of lawyers and physicians and scientists? After all, it's not just blue-collar jobs that can be done abroad: magnetic imaging can be analyzed by radiologists in Malaysia. The same applies to outsourcing due diligence, say, to attorneys in Romania. Moreover, whether at home or abroad, documents and spreadsheets can be deciphered, and medical tests analyzed, as accurately by software as they can by human beings.

Much has been said and written about how more of the nation's income has been ascending to the top 1 percent and even smaller slivers of that tier. That is altogether true. Yet it's also important to note that a by no means small segment of Americans has been doing quite well. Fully 28 percent of all households came away with $100,000 or more in 2016. At the top one-fifth of households—some 25 million families plus individuals living alone—the *bottom* income was a comfortable $121,000.

While most workers' wages have stayed stagnant, that isn't true for the top fifth. If we again look back to 1973, using 2015-value dollars, the top fifth began at a more modest $86,000. So its current $121,000 is 41 percent higher. Indeed, due to this upward flow of dollars to the top one-fifth, the remaining four-fifths now have smaller shares of the pie.

Thus far, these top one-in-five of American households have been shielded from the wage malaise. This tier provides a solid phalanx of voters who may be amenable to Republican policies. So it is in the party's interest to keep this tier contented and comfortable. The party of the very wealthy needs an adjacent buffer as political buttress.

Terrorists are blending in with refugees, even after the examples in France and Germany show the danger. (Indiana)

CONSERVATIVE OR POPULIST: NEITHER OR BOTH?

Conservatism: Canon and Camouflage

As an undergraduate, my favorite subject was political philosophy, which I first pursued at the University of St. Andrews in Scotland. A fellow student of mine was Russell Kirk, who went on to write his masterful *The Conservative Mind*.[1] Much inspired by Kirk, I embarked on a book of my own, which featured an admiring analysis of Edmund Burke. It was Burke's eloquence and intellect that gave conservatism a footing as enduring as the liberalism of John Locke and eclipsing the collectivism of Karl Marx.

For most of its history, the Republican Party has characterized its principles and policies as conservative. Indeed, it would be hard to find any of its officials—the current president excluded—who haven't applied that appellation to themselves.

In meditative moments, party notables will add Burke into the conversation. They will avow that the exercise of power, to be legitimate, must have a philosophical basis. Burke's precepts come from his seminal *Reflections on the Revolution in France*, which was published in 1790, concurrent with the adoption of our own Constitution. To conservatives, and many others, they remain as relevant as this nation's founding charter. As Burke himself would say, some ideas are timeless.

The science does not support that climate change is all man-made. (Texas)

161

CLASSICAL CONSERVATISM, ACCORDING TO EDMUND BURKE[2]

- History consists for the greater part of the miseries brought upon the world by pride, ambition, avarice, revenge, lust, sedition, hypocrisy, ungoverned zeal, and all the traits of disorderly appetites which shake the public.
- The inclinations of men should frequently be thwarted, their will controlled, and their passions brought into subjection.
- It is with infinite caution that any man ought to venture upon pulling down an edifice, which has answered in tolerable degree the common purposes of society.
- Society is . . . a partnership not only between those who are living, but between those who are living, those who are dead, and those who are to be born . . . which holds all physical and all moral natures, each in their appointed place.
- The characteristic essence of property is to be unequal . . . The body of the people . . . must respect that property of which they cannot partake.
- It has been the misfortune . . . of this age, that everything is to be discussed, as if the Constitution of our country were to be always a subject of altercation rather than enjoyment.
- We know, and it is our pride to know, that man is by his constitution a religious animal; that atheism is not only against our reason, but our instincts; and that it cannot long prevail.

What follows will inquire how far the party's current penchants and policies are grounded in conservative tenets. In Chapter 14, I remarked on a proclivity of journalists and other commentators. When discussing the Supreme Court, they identify four of its members as the "liberal" wing and the other five as the "conservative" side. It's a way of saying that our jurists sit aloof from the swirl of partisan politics, and frame their decisions only by principle.

I can't handle how crazy some liberals are. (New Jersey)

My own preference, as I noted, is to call them Democrats and Republicans, not because of the presidents who picked them, but to highlight their partisan leadings.

This said, I will now try to accommodate both those journalists and myself by creating conjoint party-ideology designations for the current Court's majority. In this chapter, they will be called *Republican Conservatives*. There's a reason for this reconciliation (*Democratic Liberals* must wait for another book).

The reason is that this trope helps to display some parameters of Republican conservatism. Here's how: each time the five Republican members assemble to effect a decision, they are putting a conservative stamp on the outcome they have chosen. Thus:

- Lower pay for women must be considered conservative, because that disparity was affirmed by the Republican-Conservative members in *Ledbetter v. Goodyear Tire and Rubber (2007)*.
- Allowing freer rein for gun ownership must be considered conservative, because it was affirmed by the Republican-Conservative members in *District of Columbia v. Heller (2008)*.
- Permitting corporations greater leeway in fund candidates and elections must be considered conservative, because that was affirmed by the Republican-Conservative members in *Citizens United v. Federal Election Commission (2010)*.
- Letting states disenfranchise citizens if they miss a few elections must be considered conservative, because that was affirmed by the Republican-Conservative members in *Husted v. A. Philip Randolph Institute (2018)*.
- Agreeing that states can contort legislative maps so that fewer voters end up with most of the seats must be considered conservative, because such maneuvering was affirmed by the Republican-Conservative members in *Rucho v. Common Cause (2019)*.

Indeed, if later this year, the five decree that a president's tax returns cannot be examined for fact-finding purposes, that policy must also be considered conservative, because it will be handed down by the Republican-Conservative members.

People feel Republicans are racist, just because they want people to work for a living.
(Florida)

Do these judicial actions help toward understanding Republican conservatism? Here, we have to do better than Humpty-Dumpty's declaration: "When *I* use a word, it means just what I choose it to mean."[3] More suitable is what my sociological colleagues call "operational definitions." Instead of crafting an elegant paragraph, they suggest going and looking at whatever it is in action. For instance, go and observe the meetings of several school boards. At the end, you'll have a pretty good definition of what they are and do.

That's essentially what we did by watching the Supreme Court. Those five bullet points listed above can serve as steps toward fathoming a party's ideology. True, thus far we haven't learned what is conservative about countenancing gerrymandering. What wasn't mentioned is that Republican lawmakers are more apt to pursue this practice. Does this mean the jurists were acting as Republicans, rather than as conservatives? Needless to say, they would take offense at such a suggestion.

Parts of the party's platform can also be set alongside conservative principles.

Life. Every Republican candidate, from president to township treasurer, is expected to affirm that all pregnancies are hallowed and must be carried to completion. So what needs elaboration is how viewing humanity as starting so very early has a conservative foundation. After all, individuals of all political hues are shocked by wanton killings, and would prefer a world where they do not occur.

Many individuals who are not conservatives display at least an equal concern for life. This is particularly true of those who oppose capital punishment. On this premise, the most vicious murderer, even if fully proved guilty, should be spared from execution. If nothing else, there may be a virtuous human being within him, as often emerges after twenty years behind bars. Interestingly, most Republicans reject that reasoning. They want to retain and deploy the death penalty, a stance that is avidly led by the current attorney general, William Barr.

One rationale is that the abhorrence of abortion has a historic lineage. Honoring wisdom from the past is a prime conservative tenet. But, as was discussed in Chapter 20, moves to ban abortion have fairly recent origins. For

---

I had an abortion. The guilt was terrible. (Florida)

centuries, the Roman Catholic Church countenanced the ending of pregnancies until physical movement could be felt. It was only just after the American Civil War that the Church's current stance was codified. Evangelical churches were permissive or ambiguous as recently as the early 1970s. Conservatism, quite literally, is about *conserving* principles and practices that have proved their merit by enduring the tests of time. By that touchstone, *Roe v. Wade (1973)* now has as long a lineage as the opposition of abortion by the Southern Baptist Convention.

Firearms. The private ownership of lethal weapons is grounded in custom and tradition. The Pilgrims brought rifles over on the *Mayflower*, alongside their bibles and prayer books. Henry Wadsworth Longfellow's "embattled farmers" who faced British troops at Bunker Hill carried their own arms into battle. And, of course, thanks to an interpretation by five Republican-Conservative jurists, the Constitution now allows military-level weaponry in every American closet.

But the Second Amendment was reinterpreted by happenstance. Guns weren't high on the founders' minds, even if militias were. Under slightly different circumstances, bearing arms might never have made it to the Bill of Rights. So what might be another conservative case for allowing private firepower? A place to start is with the first reason most owners give: the elemental need for self-defense. In this case, it is another application of the "right to life," but here it is one's own life and the lives of persons near and dear. Citizens need guns in their homes and vehicles, places of business, and on their persons, because our society is rife with ruffians with an avidity for violence. No one will deny that ensuring personal safety is a primary concern. Given this logic, a private armory is simply another purchase, not different from sturdy locks or electronic alarms. So it isn't clear why the choice of one particular product rises to the height of a principle tenet of the party. Or if it does, why it should be specified as conservative.

Other reasons for privately owning firearms are the ability to form modern citizen militias, with a readiness to repel foreign invaders, and being armed so as to be able to resist officials of one's own country who use their powers despotically. Invoking the muskets of yore is a Republican variant of approved civil

---

I dislike excuses and playing the victim. This country is becoming so soft that no one expects to work. (Minnesota)

disobedience. Here the principle of limited government paired with advocacy of the Second Amendment can extend to organizing a force against its agents.

Homosexuality. The GOP has a quotient of gay supporters, albeit not many. Still, many in the party hold that homosexuality is neither natural nor normal. Some go further, deeming it deviant or aberrant. When it comes to sexuality in general, canons of custom and convention support the party's position. Throughout most of this nation's history, absolute heterosexuality was seen as the only tolerable designation. This is enough to give disquiet about homosexuality a conservative grounding.

But recall the reference to *custom* in the previous paragraph. At first reading, there is much to be said for sustaining practices of long duration. (Why change dining three times a day?) But that begs some questions. One is whether an ostensible custom may be unfair or unjust. In many societies, the enslavement of human beings was once construed as natural or normal, at least by those who weren't in chains. So is genital surgery in some cultures today. Or arranged marriages, where fifteen-year-olds are consigned to someone thirty years older. People can and do suffer under conditions others deem to be customary. Those who do not identify as heterosexual feel they lack full citizenship when they are barred from certain occupations or denied the benefits of marriage.

Dunes and Streams. In our dictionaries, *conservatism* stands only two letters apart from *conservation*. In fact, the movement to preserve species and safeguard the environment began with patrician Republicans like Gifford Pinchot and Theodore Roosevelt. It was Richard Nixon who installed the Environmental Protection Agency. But today, the EPA itself is on an endangered list.

Republicans now exalt the capacity of human beings to commandeer the resources of their planet. Compounding chemicals, extracting minerals, and breakthroughs with solar energy and nuclear fission have been intellectual feats that prolong life and lift living standards. At the same time, these advances often entail stripping hilltops, discarding waste in streams, and extracting gases from under farmlands. Since Ronald Reagan's presidency, these and similar incursions have never worried the GOP. Its stance is that conservationist concerns undermine profit margins, undercutting innovation and development.

The Second Amendment is essential to the pursuit of happiness. (California)

Republicans may be asked about their conservative vision for the natural world, and what principles apply. Some may hold that the planet is sturdy and will adapt to what humans inflict. Or that the warnings of scientists advance personal ideologies rather than objective study. Conservatism, in a Republican application, might argue that we can never know for certain all we would like to understand, and therefore it is better to address current needs than hypothetical scenarios.

Shrinking the State. Republicans routinely complain that government at all levels has grown too large, too powerful, too overreaching. This is all the more worrisome because the administrative state differs from other entities. Public agencies don't say *please*. Rather, they command, dictate, and decree. While conservatism is not synonymous with democracy, it holds that people can best order their own lives without official edicts.

However, in practice, this policy of decreasing government size is not imposed across the board. In many spheres, Republicans favor a strong state. Police forces should have full rein, unimpeded by constitutional niceties. Schools should be able to suspend pupils they view as unruly, without the intricacies of due process. Strict rules should be imposed on clinics whose medical or surgical services are seen as immoral or distasteful. A sturdy national defense should bring military contracts that shower payouts on executives and investors. Government guarantees to for-profit colleges should be structured so that it's the students who end in jeopardy.

Whether conservative or otherwise, Republicans have never balked at using government to redistribute income, at least when it flows in an ascending arc. They object when funds are dispatched downward, to citizens they deem undeserving. In that vein, the Republican Party bestowing largesse on its own people—say, public subsidies to a golf course—can be reconciled with its conservatism.

So for the GOP, limited government means fewer funds for the poor, less money to public health and education, and minimal budgets for frills like research and the arts. Of course, awkward moments may arise, such as when Social Security and Medicare are on the table. As they approach senior years, even self-reliant Republicans find these cushions comforting. So they tell

---

Republicans have chosen to make God's laws as basis for our laws as men. (Ohio)

themselves that what they are receiving is not government assistance, but that taxes exacted from them earlier, which prepaid for these services.

Capitalism. More Republicans favor the philosophies of Ayn Rand than Edmund Burke. Her creed centers on profits, with scant attention to posterity. Insofar as its conservatism centers on personal freedoms, coming first are those associated with business success. If Republicans cast the wealthy as their prime constituency, it is because their readiness to take risks spreads prosperity across the board.

At first glance, it may seem odd to apply the term conservative to capitalism, with its merciless markets. Analysts from Alexander Hamilton to Karl Marx have shown how this system eviscerates traditions and how its institutions give priority to profits. Even now, pharmaceutical firms are working on pills that can terminate pregnancies even more quickly and quietly than those available today. Careers take first priority, with marriages postponed and births on the decline. Elsewhere, the spread of e-commerce is subverting local stores that once bonded neighborhoods. Amid all this churning, it's hard to see what's being conserved. Earlier conservatives called for caution, contemplation, and a balance of preservation and innovation. It is hard to see how such a philosophy can be adapted for so careening an era.

Populism: Style and Substance

Among Donald Trump's many upheavals has been to resurrect a long-dormant spectacle called *populism*. Some see it as part of a worldwide phenomenon, from Venezuela and Brazil to Burma and Hungary, even a usually impassive Great Britain. If nothing else, the roaring at Trump's almost weekly rallies are displays of a populous being roused.

It would be interesting to hear the reaction of Alexander Hamilton, the progenitor of many Republican tenets. Here's a remark he inserted in *The Federalist*:

> There are citizens, who inflame the minds of the less intelligent parts of the community by saying their vanity with that unfailing specific, *all*

I get riled by the whole race thing. (Virginia)

power is seated in the people. I am not one of those who gain an influence by cajoling the unthinking mass.[4]

There can be good and bad populisms. Hence epithets like *demagogue, agitator*, or *rabble-rouser*, the latter disparaging the followers along with their leader.

It could be contended that two other presidents in living memory, Franklin Roosevelt and Ronald Reagan, solidified their administrations by populist appeals. Both presidents, of course, were widely popular. But populism involves going a step further. In particular, appealing directly to the general public, as with Roosevelt's "fireside chats" using radio, and Reagan's ever-present "morning in America." The tactic can be deployed from both the left and right.

The motif of the populism of the left is almost always a demand for the redistribution of income and wealth. "Arise, ye prisoners of starvation; arise, ye wretched of the earth!" went one refrain. Or Nebraska's William Jennings Bryan, with his call to arms, "You shall not press down on the brow of labor this crown of thorns!" Theodore Roosevelt, even as a Republican president, castigated "the malefactors of great wealth."[5]

So there's a material substance to leftward populism. Its goal is a nation both classless and egalitarian, even incorporating some aspects of socialism. Nor were figures like the two Roosevelts unusual. Both affluent at birth, they proposed measures that would subvert many of their own privileges.

But Theodore Roosevelt was an anomalous Republican. It's hard to cite even a handful of Republicans who have argued for serious economic shifts. Insofar as there is a Republican populism, it must be understood in other ways.

The first is as a *style*. And here Donald Trump has been its utmost avatar. In this respect, he differs markedly from Franklin Roosevelt. Both came into office with inherited wealth and Ivy League degrees. But Trump presents an appearance and disposition of a hurly-burly streetfighter, which in fact comes naturally to him—it is not in any way feigned. His diction and syntax, coupled with his aversion to anything of book length, would place him among what Hamilton call "the unthinking mass."

So Trump is a populist, inasmuch as his own style is genuinely consonant with those in his bellowing bleachers. No other figure on the current political

---

I disagree with homosexuality and transgender lifestyles. They are not what God intended. (Kansas)

scene, left or right, not even Bernie Sanders, comes close to his presentation. So what is his populist aim?

It certainly isn't economic reallocation. Apart from some tropes about drug prices and offshore production, hardly any shafts are hurled at leading corporations. Nor are the wealthy chosen as targets. Indeed, both large firms and the very rich were the prime beneficiaries of Trump's 2017 tax bill. In fairness, it must be noted that those at his rallies did not oppose his material priorities. Republicans of modest status have long basked in their alliance with their economic betters.

That said, populism of the right evokes other forces. In the United States, there is the desire of groups of citizens to end all abortions, to safeguard ownerships of firearms, and to halt the changing composition of the country. This populism posits that if this is what people want, then they are entitled to press their positions. Whatever occurs in this sphere, it is unlikely to discommode the wealthy side of the spectrum. Indeed, they realize such accommodations are needed to secure allies for their own agendas.

But Republican populism has other strings to its bow. One of its major shafts is to direct enmity to "elites" who are said to deride upstanding citizens. The Republican mantra says that there are supercilious academics, intellectuals, and entertainers out there who are sneering at the shortcomings of people like yourselves. The dominant cultural nexus of the country is said to disparage everyday tastes and choices. Even religious observances are patronized, as are commonplace pastimes and traditions.

The net effect, of course, is to deflect attention from another "elite." These are people who actually have power: business owners, corporate executives, and well-informed investors, who absorb an increasing fraction of the net national product. At no point does the Republican battle plan even suggest that this highly remunerated stratum warrants criticism, let alone anger. Apparently, there can be a populism which has no quarrel with prevailing distributional patterns.

So current Republican populism is a mixture of style and substance. Our current president has the talent to stir popular passions. It's impossible to visualize such enthusiasm by a President Romney or a President McCain. Yet the substance is of long standing for the Republican Party: to ally with

---

Losing the Second Amendment would only hurt law-abiding Americans, who need to be able to defend themselves. (South Carolina)

whatever causes will divert attention from the excesses of wealth and profits. Try imagining that the investment banking company, Morgan Stanley, will make a contribution to Planned Parenthood.

Every so often, journalists visit depressed regions, which have been ravaged by lost jobs, fractured families, and addiction. The journalists then note that these constituencies vote overwhelmingly Republican. Is this a paradox? A premise of democracy is that citizens know—indeed, have reflected on—their own affinities and interests. So they have concluded that what Republicans offer is preferable, in many cases by far.

Our two major parties are national, which means that they try to mobilize majorities, aiming to gain the presidency and at least one congressional chamber. (Despite 2016, the Electoral College route is still an anomaly.) So a populist posture has to cut across classes and regions.

At this point, Trump has chosen to address only those already attracted to his manner and agenda. Anyone even faintly outside his orbit can expect to suffer his lash. Given this insularity, his best effort in 2016 garnered him 46 percent of the electorate. Even losers like John Kerry and Albert Gore did better, each attaining 48 percent. Roosevelt and Reagan built truly national followings. In his second run, Roosevelt swept 61 percent of the popular vote and 98 percent of the Electoral College. Reagan almost matched him, with 59 percent and 98 percent. Roosevelt added four points between his first and second tries. Reagan did double that.

Donald Trump clearly believes that he can and will be reelected. In any playbook, he will need to enhance his 46 percent. (Going for the Electoral College again is a high-risk game.) What remains unclear is where any new votes might come from. It's probable that 2016 yielded him all the disillusioned Democrats he will ever attract. Of course, populist success depends on the compelling figure on the podium. But its ultimate measure is whether it broadens its appeal. There are no signs that Trump is finding new sources of support. On the contrary, all evidence is that his putative "base" is dwindling.

I share the values of a nation that takes pride in making our own products. (New Jersey)

NOVEMBER 3, 2020

By some measures, the economy is doing quite well. At this writing, the stock market is still booming, although it's not certain how far this resounds with many voters. Donald Trump's most frequent assertion is that the workforce is about as close to full employment is as it can be, and has reached its current high under his administration. Anyone who wants a job can find one. If all this is true, why would people want a different president?

Vladimir O. Key, the past century's most distinguished political scientist, once opined, "Voters are not fools."[1] They may not be up on developments in Taiwan and Syria—or, for that matter, the fine print in trade agreements. But they are very much aware of their own situations. And here's what they know about those new jobs.

To start, they know that many jobs don't offer more than subsistence pay. There are plenty of openings at Lyft and Uber, where you're only paid when you're transporting passengers. McDonald's and Taco Bell are also hiring, but they are not offering patently higher pay. If Amazon is a top employer, most of its positions are in warehouses, snatching products off shelves and packing them in boxes. Facebook and Google may be cutting-edge companies, but most of their new hires are contract workers, often on short-term assignments and with limited benefits. In higher education, a field I know well, just about the only openings are for impecunious adjuncts. Many teach classes at several colleges in an attempt to pay their bills. This is the current economy for millions of Americans.

There's also a real shortage of affordable housing that middling households can manage, with some people devoting at least half their income to that basic

---

I believe in Right to Life and the Second Amendment and holding teachers accountable for poor performance. (Michigan)

need. For those who are repaying student loans, even the amount on their checks are illusory. These difficulties are part of the reason why people aren't having children, or are stopping at one. True, families with two incomes, now the norm, aren't "poor." But at least some linger at uncongenial jobs, because they'd be bereft without the health insurance. A frequent pitch by incumbents is "You're doing better than ever!" It's not clear that this resounds with a plurality of the voting public.

An ace sitting presidents have is the "October surprise," contrived to impel voters to think that it is best not to change. One problem for Donald Trump is his penchant for devising crises, whether over Iran or Venezuela or North Korea. By this time Americans have become so jaded that a furtive October shock won't stick. Indeed, he made such a foray in October 2018, when he mounted a last-minute effort to retain his Republican majority in the House. His story was that a full-scale invasion was on its way via Mexico, so menacing that several thousand troops had to be rapidly dispatched. Voters not only didn't tremble; they changed the composition of the House.

To win again, Donald Trump will have to add to the 62,692,411 total he attained in 2016. The reason is that this time, any Democrat will finish with considerably more than Hillary Clinton's 65,667,168. Up toward 70 million is not implausible. That add-on will obviate an Electoral College debacle. The president's difficulty is his combined unwillingness and incapacity to appeal to citizens outside his immediate orbit. Much is made of his raucous rallies. And it's true that none of his competitors have been to assemble so fervid a core. Think Cruz, Rubio, Kasich, Clinton. (So far, he hasn't gone head to head with Sanders.)

Gauged by Republican votes in 2018's House races, his following was down to 50,467,181. Earlier chapters, on midterms and special elections, showed that large numbers of his 2016 supporters were staying at home. In 2020, he will need to bring out at least every single one of the 12,225,230 who skipped 2018.

That said, his challenge will be finding additional supporters. It strains the mind to wonder where they might come from. Unlike other presidents, Trump has not sought to construe his constituency as nationwide. He has avoided public meetings, seldom delivers addresses over television, and holds hardly any press conferences. By his measures, he may be doing fine with those who are

---

I am for beefing up the military to keep America secure from terrorists. (Florida)

already converted. Indeed, he fires them up—not least through Twitter—by casting his opponents in the grossest of terms. The other party is always the "Dems," its leader is "Crazy Nancy," his erstwhile opponent is still "Crooked Hillary." Is that how to lure in the undecideds he would need for another term?

All campaigns conjure visions of independent voters, who might be enticed to join their side. That worked with Dwight Eisenhower and Ronald Reagan, as well as in Bill Clinton's second bid and Barack Obama's first. It didn't in 2016, when Hillary Clinton fantasized that suburban Republicans might switch to her. But Trump's current campaign has yet to identify individuals who are still equivocal or ambivalent. There's no way he can win unless he does.

And then there are dirty tricks. It's not whether one or another of these deceptions swings an election. As in much of life, we don't know which of many grains will ultimately tip a scale. Given the welter of advertisements and other messages on television and the Internet, it's doubtful that some interference from Russia would grab more than a modicum of attention. And even given Russia's technological savvy, an amateur grasp of the American vernacular makes the foreign source apparent.

Interestingly, the same holds for new internet strategies Republicans claim to be contriving. True, they've had successes in the past, notably the "Willie Horton" scare, used in George H. W. Bush's 1988 campaign. What's different this year is that there are no signs that Republican tacticians know how to appeal to people who are putatively in the middle. Even if they assemble focus groups, they have to keep both eyes on the Oval Office. How would their principal react to banners that don't shout unwavering loyalty to him?

And it's not just Donald Trump who is up for reelection. Voters are being asked to bestow their approval on the entire apparatus of the Republican Party. The cast includes Mitch McConnell and William Barr, Betsy DeVos and Stephen Miller, Pat Cipollone and Eugene Scalia, Wilbur Ross and Kellyanne Conway. Not to mention that their administration chose Neil Gorsuch and Brett Kavanaugh. It isn't easy to visualize majority support for these and other enablers.

The president's single legislative success was his "Tax Cuts and Jobs Act," enacted in his first year of office. The best index of its popular support was that the senators who passed it secured their seats from 45 percent of the voting

---

Republicans support private companies that make the country grow. (Florida)

public. (With the same template, Gorsuch and Kavanaugh both had 46 percent.)

This November's ballots will show how the nation assesses the president's postures on economics and immigration, the state of the planet and social policy, and his hostility to alliances and his interventions abroad. His rallies vouch that his stalwarts are still on his side. November will hear from less boisterous Americans.

All told, the Republicans' candidates have placed second in six of the last seven presidential races. Indeed, the most recent year their choice won was in 2004, when George W. Bush attained a second term. (Two years later, he completely lost the House and the Senate.) In politics, a lot is possible. Two upsets were Harry Truman's reelection and Donald Trump's bombshell four years ago. The prime reason for the latter was so many Democrats stayed at home. If 2018 signaled anything, it was their remorse. They showed up for those midterms in numbers only matched back in 1932. This November, they'll be out in force again, no matter who their party nominates. Indeed, the margins will be so high that even an Electoral College end-run won't work. Every indicator in this book shows—and this is its last word—that there aren't enough Americans to give Donald John Trump a second term.

I believe in a strong military, secure borders, and a country with law and order. Immigrants are welcome, but they should be forced to become an American in its entirety. (Virginia)

ENDNOTES

Of all nations, by far, the United States maintains the most reliable collations of election information. These are the foremost compendiums, which were indispensable for this book.

- *The Almanac of American Politics* (Columbia Books and Information Services). This magisterial compilation—the current edition runs to 2,043 pages—has been available since 1972. For example, it can tell you that in Illinois's 15th congressional district, 80 percent of its Trump voters turned out for the 2018 midterms, whereas 95 percent of its Democrats did.

- *Statistics of the Congressional Election* (Office of the Clerk, US House of Representatives). This collation goes back to 1920, is free online and is easy to use. It also includes complete figures for presidential and congressional races. Among other things, it aggregates the 2018 votes for New Jersey's twelve congressional districts, so we can see that the Democrats' total was 1,856,819, against 1,298,664 for the Republicans.

- *US Election Atlas*, also free and online, has voting figures for president, senator, and governors, all the way back to 1824. (That year, Andrew Jackson defeated John Quincy Adams, 151,363 to 113,141.) More recently, you can learn that in all 2018 races for governor, Democratic candidates got 46,298,981 votes, against Republicans' 43,476,882.

- *Ballotpedia*. This celebrated service provides figures that can't be found anywhere else. For example, a Texas special election, where only 35,024 people showed up. Or the lineup on the state supreme courts whose members run on partisan labels.

- *United States Election Project*. Every two years, this University of Florida service computes the precise size of the potential electorate. In 2018, altogether 235,714,420 citizens were legally qualified, of whom

118,581,921 did vote. We can learn that the 2016 pool was 8.4 percent larger than in 2008, so that tweaking is needed if we want to compare the two turnout totals.

- *National Election Pool*, managed by Edison Research. This service, which has been operating since 2004, interviews people as they leave the polls. It focuses on personal characteristics, to show how voters divide for candidates and parties. Its findings are on CNN's website. In 2018, its sample ran to 75,836, more than enough for reliable results, even for smaller subgroups. Hence we learn that 54 percent of unmarried men opted for Democratic candidates, as did 73 percent of Latina women. Also reported was that 61 percent of Republicans said they owned guns, while 64 percent of Democrats don't.
- Two polling organizations warrant inclusion: the *Pew Research Center* and the *Public Religion Research Institute*. Both are notable for posing questions that delve beneath the surface. Thus the Pew Center asked people if they felt colleges "have a negative effect" in this country. Among Republicans, 64 percent agreed, versus 21 percent of Democrats. The Religion Institute prepared a statement saying that white people now suffer more discrimination than other groups. With Republicans, 74 percent agreed, against 30 percent of Democrats.

Chapter 1

1. Alan Abramowitz, "The Trump Effect," in Larry Sabato and Kyle Kondrik, *The Blue Wave* (Roman & Littlefield, 2019).
2. For reams of important information, see Stanley Greenberg, *R.I.P. G.O.P. How the New America is Dooming the Republicans* (Thomas Dunne, 2019).
3. "Birth Expectations of US Women," National Center for Health Statistics, October 2016. A third of women aged 35–44 who are now childless do not expect to have one. Nearly half of women with one child do not expect to have another.
4. See Richard Hasen, *Plutocrats United* (Yale University Press, 2016): "money does not buy votes or elections."
5. "Somebody Just Put a Price Tag on the 2016 Election," *Washington Post*, April 14, 2017.

Chapter 2

1. There's an exception. By custom, if not inertia, vice presidents have had automatic access to the nomination. Richard Nixon, Gerald Ford, and George H. W. Bush all took this route in the GOP. So did Lyndon Johnson, Hubert Humphrey, Walter Mondale, and Albert Gore among the Democrats. Only Johnson won a second full term. Michael Pence can dream.
2. See Jane Mayer's indispensable *Dark Money* (Penguin Random House, 2016).
3. Jonathan Allen and Amie Barnes, *Shattered* (Crown, 2017).

Chapter 4

1. But see "An Examination of the 2016 Electorate, Based n Validated Voters," Pew Research Center, August 9, 2018, which found that of 2012 Democrats, only 5 percent had switched to Trump, while 4 percent of 2012 Republicans turned to Clinton.
2. See Tim Alberta, *American Carnage* (Harper Collins, 2019): "It wasn't that Trump turned out historic numbers of blue collar whites, he simply won a far higher share of them than past Republicans had . . . These voters had been trending toward the GOP for a generation, and Trump's candidacy was a known accelerant."

Chapter 6

1. See Sam Wang, "Democrats would have had to win the popular vote by 7 percentage points to take control of the House the way that districts are now," "The Great Gerrymander of 2012," *New York Times,* February 2, 2013. Plus Charles Cook, "Demographic developments cast doubt on whether even a 2006-size wave would enable Democrats to win control of the House at any point in this decade," "The GOP Keeps Getting Whiter," *National Journal*, March 16, 2013.
2. "To Beat Trump, Focus on Corruption," *New York Times*, November 3, 2019.
3. Ashley Rae Goldenberg, "Only 37% of Americans Can Name Their Congressman," Media Research Center, June 5, 2017.

Chapter 8

1. "How Different Groups Voted in Alabama," *Washington Post*, December 13, 2017.

2. There was a reason for miniscule turnouts in Texas: the winner would serve for only six months. In fact, primaries had already been held to choose candidates for oncoming full term.

3. See the lament of John Whitbeck, Virginia Republican chairman: "We spend a ton of money trying to get Trump voters engaged, and [they] didn't vote in these off year elections." "Under a Cloud, Trump is Still Unyielding," *New York Times*, December 20, 2019.

Chapter 9

1. Theodore Arrington, "Gerrymandering the House, 1972–2016," Larry J. Sabato's Crystal Ball, November 26, 2018.

Chapter 11

1. Of the twenty current senators from the ten smallest states, twelve are Republicans and eight are Democrats.

2. See David Wasserman, "In 2020, it's possible Trump could win 5 million fewer votes than this opponent, and still win a second term," NBC News, July 19, 2019.

Chapter 12

1. "What's stronger than a Blue Wave?" *New York Times*, November 29, 2018.

2. See Andrew Hacker, "US House Elections are Equally Unfair," Bloomberg Politics, January 24, 2019.

3. Chief Justice John Roberts for the Republicans: "We conclude that partisan gerrymandering claims present political questions beyond the reach of the federal courts." Quoted in "Court, Ruling 5–4, Gives Green Light to Gerrymander," *New York Times*, June 28, 2019.

Chapter 13

1. It wasn't always this way. From 1932 through 1994, Democrats controlled the Senate for fifty of those sixty-two years. Even popularly elected Republicans—Dwight Eisenhower, Richard Nixon, Ronald Reagan, George H. W. Bush—didn't have a supportive upper chamber through all of their tenures.

Chapter 14

1. "State Supreme Court Elections," Ballotopedia, 2019. In the states' 49 seats, Republicans have 32 and Democrats 17. The courts in Texas and Alabama are totally Republican, while New Mexico, Illinois, Pennsylvania, and West Virginia have Democratic majorities.
2. In an earlier oral argument, Chief Justice Roberts dismissed proposed remedies as "a bunch of baloney" and "sociological gobbledygook."

Chapter 16

1. Still, the 2018 midterms had Democrats ending with only 47 percent of all state seats, despite winning 55 percent of two-party votes nationwide. See annual compilations by the National Conference of State Legislatures.
2. See Jill Lapore's deft exegesis in *These Truths* (Norton, 2019): "Either abortion was murder and guns meant freedom, or guns meant murder and abortion was freedom."
3. Alan Abramowitz, *The Great Alignment* (Yale University Press, 2018).

Chapter 17

1. Jason Le Miere, "Is Trump Republican?" *Newsweek,* September 7, 2014.

Chapter 18

1. The Pew Research Center asked people if it bothered them "a lot" that some wealthy people don't pay their fair tax shares. Of Democrats, 79 percent said they were, while 37 percent of Republicans were not. On whether they felt business corporations make "too much profits," 72 percent of Democrats felt that way, and 38 percent of Republicans didn't. "Growing Partisan Divide Over Fairness of the Nation's Tax System," April 4, 2019.

Chapter 19

1. "Americans' Views on Masculinity," Pew Research Center, January 23, 2019.
2. "Prevalence of Obesity Among Adults and Youth, 2015–2016," National Center for Health Statistics, October 2017.

Chapter 20

1. "Should abortion be legal or illegal in most or cases?" Pew Research Center, October 2018.

2. Ed Stetzer, "Pro-Choice Evangelicals?" https://www.christianitytoday.com /edstetzer/2012/november/morning-roundup-11512-pro-choice-evangelicals -president.html.

3. Southern Baptist Convention Resoluton on Abortion. St. Louis, Missouri, 1971. http://www.sbc.net/resolutions/13/resolution-on-abortion.

4. James Unnever, "God Imagery and Opposition to Abortion and Capital Punishment," *Sociology of Religion.* Vol. 71, 307–377.

Chapter 21

1. "Do You Personally Identify as LGBT?" Gallup, May 2018.

2. Gallup's question, posed in May 2018, was: "Do you think marriages between same sex couples should or should not be recognized by the law as valid and with the same rights as traditional marriages?"

Chapter 22

1. See Nancy Isenberg, *White Trash* (Penguin Random House, 2016).

Chapter 23

1. The president apparently shares this sentiment, having been heard to say, "laziness is a trait in blacks. I really believe it." Quoted in John O'Donnell, *Trumped: The Inside Story of the Real Donald Trump* (Simon & Schuster, 1991).

2. See Noel Ignatiev, *How the Irish Became White* (Routledge, 1995).

3. "Births: Final Data for 2018," National Vital Statistics Reports, November 2019.

4. "How Americans See the State of Race Relations," Pew Research Center, April 9, 2019, which prepared the statement, "There is too much attention paid to race and race relations in our country these days." Among Republicans, 75 percent agreed, while only 21 percent of Democrats did.

5. The Pew Research Center asked white respondents if they felt that "blacks are treated less fairly in hiring, pay, and promotions." Of white Democrats, 72 percent agreed, versus 21 percent of white Republicans. "Race in America," April 2019.

6. "One Nation Divided Under Trump," Public Religion Research Institute, 2017. American Values Study.

7. The Public Religion Research Institute prepared this statement: "Immigrants are invading our country and replacing our culture." Among Republicans, 63 percent agreed, against 29 percent of Democrats. "Fractured Nation: Widening Partisan Polarization and Key Issues in 2020 President Elections," October 2019.

Chapter 24

1. Only seven members took part in this case. The vacancy due to Justice Scalia's death had not yet been filled, and Justice Kagan recused herself because she had worked on the case when she was Solicitor General.
2. Justice Alito added, "The University of Texas can pick and choose which racial and ethnic groups it would like to favor."
3. Clarence Thomas concedes that he entered Yale Law School under a preferential program. Here's how he put it in *My Grandfather's Son* (Harper Collins 2007): "minority students were admitted under the same standards as these . . . privileged white kids . . . from wealthy families, or had parents who'd gone to Yale."
4. Richard Reeves and Christopher Pulliam, "No Room at the Top," Brookings Institution, February 2019.

Chapter 25

1. "The Growing Partisan Divide in Views of Higher Education," Pew Research Center, August 18, 2019.
2. Pew Research Center, "Republicans' Views on Evolution," January 2014.
3. "Partisan Flash Points in Public's View of Global Threats," Pew Research Center, July 30, 2019.
4. Also see Gallup's March 2015 report titled, "College Educated Republicans Most Skeptical of Global Warming."

Chapter 26

1. See Stephen Witt, "Big Guns," *New York,* November 14–27, 2016 : "Somewhere between 20 and 30 percent of Americans owned guns . . . 3 percent owned more than half the country's guns . . . on average, 17 different firearms."

2. "CBS News Poll: American Attitudes toward Gun Violence." CBS News, CBS Interactive, 5 Dec. 2017, www.cbsnews.com/news/cbs-news-poll-americans-attitudes-to-gun-violence-sandy-hook-newtown-anniversary/.

3. "Where Democrats and Republicans Agree, Differ on Gun Policy," Pew Research Center, June 23, 2017. Some other owners are Donald Trump, with a DT Heckler & Koch revolver, and Lindsey Graham, who keeps an AR-15 semiautomatic rifle. "GOP Candidates and Mass Shootings," *New York Times*, August 3, 2015.

4. Quoted in Craig Whitney, *Living with Guns* (Public Affairs, 2012).

5. "Deaths: Final Data for 2017." National Vital Statistics Reports, June 2019.

6. Michael Nutter quoted in *New York Times*, "Daily Gun Violence Echoes Across U.S." May 23, 2016

7. See note 2 above. Also see the 2018 CNN exit poll showing that 77 percent of Democrats support stricter gun controls, and an exactly equal 77 percent of Republicans don't.

Chapter 27

1. "Senate Defeats Treaty 49 to 35," *New York Times*, March 19, 1920.

2. Quoted in William Nester, *The Jeffersonian Vision, 1801–1815* (Potomac Books, 2013).

3. *Federalist No. 36.*

4. *Federalist No. 11.*

Chapter 28

1. Megan McArdle, "The Politics of Prevarication," *Atlantic* (August 2009).

2. "Six Million Lost Voters," The Sentencing Project, October 2006.

3. For oral arguments, see "Supreme Court Weighs Ohio's Purge of Voting Rolls," *New York Times*, January 11, 2018. For the decision, see "Supreme Court, in 5-to-4 Ruling, Upholds Ohio's Bid to Purge Voter Rolls," *New York Times,* June 12, 2018.

4. For sources of license figures, which are still relevant, see Andrew Hacker, "The Price of Being Black," *New York Review of Books* (September 25, 2008).

5. Rudy Mehrbani, "Heritage Fraud Database: an Assessment," Brennan Center for Justice, September 2017. Also see Ari Berman, "Texas' Voter Registration Laws are Straight Out of the Jim Crow Playbook," *The Nation*, October 6, 2016.

Chapter 29

1. Russell Kirk, *The Conservative Mind* (Regnery, 1953).
2. Edmund Burke, *Reflections on the Revolution in France* (Dent, 1910). Originally published in 1790. For the best current analysis, see Joel Aberbach, *Understanding Contemporary American Conservatism* (Routledge, 2017).
3. Lewis Carroll, *Through the Looking Glass* (Penguin, 1994). Originally published in 1872.
4. Alexander Hamilton, op.ed. column in *The Daily Advertiser,* October 1787.
5. Speech by Theodore Roosevelt, in Provincetown, MA, August 1907. Speech by William Jennings Bryan in Chicago, at the Democratic National Convention, July 1896.

Chapter 30

1. V. O. Key Jr., *Public Opinion and American Democracy* (Knopf, 1961).